A History of Hatfield Heath

A Village Celebration for the Millennium

AD 2000

Published by the Hatfield Heath History Group

with the

Patronage of the Hatfield Heath Parish Council

ISBN 0 953 5753 06

First published 1999

Typeset by Diane Parker

Printed by Steans Printers Ltd

No part of this publication may be reproduced without the written permission of the publishers

Contents

Foreword by Mrs I Delderfield JP, District Councillor (1976-1999) v

Introduction vii

Acknowledgements ix

Bibliography xi

1. Early History 1

11. The Churches 23

111. The Schools 33

1V. The Twentieth Century 49

V. Some Buildings of Historic Interest and Local Trade & Industry 75

V1. Village Organisations. 83

Foreword

By Mrs I Delderfield, District Councillor JP, (1976 - 1999)

Firstly, congratulations to everyone concerned with the publication of 'A History of Hatfield Heath'. It is very comprehensive and has taken many hours of research, collating and recording the evolution of this village as it has developed over the years.

When I realised that the team was trying to record the names of everyone who had had any part of the social life of the Heath I imagined it could be tedious, but to the contrary - names are important and everyone mentioned has made a contribution to create a living example of what I consider a friendly completely integrated village. Different interests have been enthusiastically pursued; we have all been drawn in, welcomed and made lasting friends through work, hobbies and shared skills. Newcomers have been encouraged to join clubs and associations and have been welcomed by the two churches. In fact something for everyone, with our Parish Council working hard improving and helping to maintain the beauty of the countryside with the verging of the quality of life and work.

Hatfield Heath has a heart and it is due to the sometimes quite seemingly small and unimportant contributions of every single person mentioned herein. Read and enjoy the efforts of the latest residents who have so diligently and painstakingly written down the contributions made by all those inhabitants of the Heath.

It was not always so - When we moved from London it was very different. We were Londoners who had survived the bombing and were very excited when we had the chance of moving out of a devastated capital into a small brand new house - one of five allowed at Hatfield Heath. Country air, fresh vegetables and fruit etc.. I could not wait .... But the reality was a shock. The Heath fifty years ago had become depopulated when the war ended. The 'visitors' e.g. Americans from their bases, evacuees from London and POW's, then went home. It was a time of change and starting again. Many of the village lads did not come back and many of the girls had found life beyond Hatfield Heath and did not return. The once thriving shops were depleted, rationing was still in force. We missed the street lights of London and knew nobody. The village was not accustomed to new residents and saw no reason to accept strangers. All unaware of this we arrived on 27th October

1947. The move was quite disastrous - The removal van became stuck in the mud for the house was built on the edge of a field where corn had been growing the year before. No trees, no car or garage, no porch and very few cupboards. The pram had to be pulled into the kitchen to have the wheels washed from mud. I had a son of four, a baby of three months and a dog. There was no one to look after them while I went to Bishop's Stortford or did any shopping. To say I was lonely was an understatement. My husband travelled to London to his office by the early train that arrived at Liverpool Street at 8.00am. (Steam trains always seemed late). He would cycle to Sawbridgeworth and arrived home at about 8.00 pm. My outings were a windy walk to the village stores for food. Everyone grew their own vegetables and nobody called to welcome me or to tell me that one could buy vegetables at Mr Caton's by the mill, although that was a long walk on a November day with two children.

The only two people who came to see me were the Congregational minister the Rev. Lawton and the Rev. Horsey and believe me they were welcome. The Rev. Horsey owned an Austin 7 car that was very erratic! When it would not start he 'scooted' it along and being tall it certainly was a funny sight. (This was 'Charlie', now restored and in the possession of John White on the Chelmsford Road. Ed.) He chugged around the back, over the field, parked it by my back door then came in, put his cigarette out and asked if I was C of E. When I said yes and that I had recently been confirmed in St. Paul's Cathedral he asked me to bring my son Jim to Sunday School. From that time on I gradually become used to village life but it took a long time. The winter was cold and bleak, the Heath itself windswept and deserted, few people, few shops and, more important, nobody to say 'hello'. We were the first new residents, the other four houses empty and awaiting purchase.

The churches helped enormously as both Holy Trinity and the Chapel were the hub of the village social life. Money raising events, whist drives, Sunday school, bazaars, fetes and not forgetting the mother's union, young wives, scouts and guides.

Let us hope that the Hatfield Heath residents of the future will also make their contribution, and that our village will continue to be the warm caring place we know and love.

Introduction

The original idea of producing a book on the history of Hatfield Heath was more or less suggested simultaneously by the Conservation Group and the Village Magazine.

An initial meeting was held in September 1997 with Leslie Towers in the Chair and Breda May - Magazine Editor, Ivan Wybrew - Treasurer and the Village Archivist, Dorothy Search in attendance. Since then, a working party calling itself the Hatfield Heath History Group has met bi- monthly to define objectives, check progress and exchange information. The necessary tasks of research, interviews, writing, proofing, etc. has been undertaken by group members and after much hard work the final drafts and illustrations were available for printing in September 1999.

The agreed objective was to produce a book recording the history of the village as part of the Millennium celebrations, the merit of which we must leave the reader to judge. There is however another important consideration in that we would like to think that this small volume will, in the years to come, be read by future village residents and therefore the names of many of the people who lived, worked and contributed to the life of Hatfield Heath over the centuries, up to the year 2000, would be acknowledged in print. Who knows, perhaps in the year 3000 someone will be encouraged to update the next 1000 years!.

A considerable effort has been made to ensure that the facts given are correct with many interviews sought, and with much research undertaken. It is not intended that this book should be a definitive history of this village but rather a celebration of a numeric milestone in our history. The editors and most of those involved in the production of this book had no previous experience in this type of work. They have done their best but if anyone feels they, their family, or any significant facts have been left out or not given due weight, we can only at this stage apologise and perhaps make amends in a later edition.

Leslie G. Towers - Chairman & Joint Editor
Liz Wright - Secretary & Joint Editor
Ivan Wybrew - Treasurer & Joint Editor
Dorothy Search - Village Archivist
Hatfield Heath History Group

5th November 1999

Acknowledgements

The Hatfield Heath History Group wish to express their most sincere thanks to the following people who have made invaluable contributions towards the publication of this Book.

Ivan Wybrew: for research and writing chapters I, II, and IV.

Don Foster: for research and writing chapter III.

Leslie Towers: for research and writing chapter V.

and the following writers of chapter VI.

Ernie Field, Jim Coe, Ivan Wybrew, and Sandra Saban. - Royal British Legion

Jean Piercy - Welcome Club.

Jean Piercy, Barbara Jenkins, Jean Wybrew - Women's Institute.

Margaret Lines, Jane Newbould - Pre-School Group.

Richard Barnett - Cricket Club.

Richard Barnett - Gardening Club.

Andy Lines, David Brown - Football Club.

Jean Foster   - Heath Players.

Cliff Burnside - WEA.

Bob Parker - Bridge Club.

Brian Bland - Bowls Club.

Liz Wright - for Computer input, Research and Editing

Dorothy Search: for information, documents, illustrations, advice and overall encouragement throughout the project.

Jim and Pauline Coe: for undertaking interviews, information, illustrations and investigation work over the past two years.

Bob and Diane Parker, Ernie Fields and Breda May: for technical advice and assistance.

Ken Bennison, Pam and David Tyler and Brian Bland for advice and encouragement and most importantly the Hatfield Heath Parish Council for financial backing.

Joy Passfield: for checking facts and text.

Tony Jenkins & PBM Printing for photocopying and binding facilities.

Tim Potter and Roland Strutt for checking Chapter II.

John Clements for checking Chapter III.

Jai Chaudhuri for the cover water colour painting, and the Village Hall Trust for the back cover print.

and the following for contributions and checking facts:-

Herbert Maskell. Geoff Smith. Olive Mays. Joan Roberts. Howard Pyle. John Clements. Peter and Margaret Lines. Frank Walsh. Irene and Frank Delderfield. Kingsley James. Howard Gunn. Richard Farr. Martin and Ann Broad. Don and Jean Foster. Mark, Judy and Alex Lemon.

The Editors would also like to thank the following villagers who contributed information and illustrations :-

Jessie Adams. Peggy Austin. Lily Barker. David Brown. Gordon Barrow, Bob Bucknell. Jean Clark. Jim and Pauline Coe. Nellie Day. Irene Delderfield. Bill Eldred. Jean Foster. Mary Halls Michael Hockley. Theo Hockley. Dinah Hutchin. (Pictures from the Gilbert Hutchin Collection). Arthur Kent. Edith Kerr. Ian and Jenny Liddell.

Peter, Margaret, and Andy Lines. Bill Matheson Ted Newman. Jean Piercy. Margaret Perry. Rol and Mary Perry. Tim Potter. David Ridgewell. Helen Rose (Dix). Joan Roberts. Hugh and Marion Scantlebury. Mick and Sandra Saban. Dorothy Search. Frances Sparrow. 'Chubby' Sapsford. The URC Elders. John White. Martin and Jean Wybrew.

Bibliography

The following publications are the principal references from which information for this book have been obtained and the Editors acknowledge and thank them for their contribution:

An Introduction to Holy Trinity
   Holy Trinity PCC.

Hatfield Heath URC History Booklet
   URC Elders

Hatfield Heath URC British School Logs
   Roland Strutt Secretary

Holy Trinity Parish Magazine
   Holy Trinity PCC

Hatfield Heath Village Magazine
   HH Village Magazine Committee

Hatfield Heath County Primary Log Books
   John Clements Head Teacher HHCPS.

Eden Lady Rookwood
   Marion Scantlebury

The Great House of Hallingbury
   Heather Cocks - Gt. Hallingbury History Soc.

Gt. Hallingbury Village
   Ernest Fields - Gt. Hallingbury History Soc.

History of Harlow
   Harlow Development Corporation.

Joseph Ashby of Tysoe
   MK Ashby London 1961

Kelly's Directory (Various additions)
  Kelly's Business Directories

The Last Forest
  Oliver Rackham

The Priory of Hatfield Regis
  Alan David Jones

Portrait of a Village School
  Alan David Jones

Prosperity and Poverty
  Dr. AFJ Brown - Essex Record Office

A Sketch Map of Economic History
  JL Gaylor and others - Geo Harrap & Co.

A Social History of England 1851 - 1990
  Francois Bedarida - Methuen & Co. Ltd.

A short account of the Antiquities of HBO
  FW Galpin MA FLS.

The Victoria History of Essex
  HA Doubleday & W Page - W Dawson & Sons

The Windmills of Essex Vol 4
  KG Farrier - Charles Skilton Ltd.

Essex Record Office Chelmsford Documents.
  The Staff

Harlow Record Office Documents
  Mr D Devine & Staff

Saffron Walden Museum Documents
  The Staff

Dr AFJ Brown's 1983 lecture to the WEA on Hatfield Heath in the 19th century.

(1)
Early History

"This shire is most fatt, fruitfull, and full of profitable things, exceeding anie other shire for the general comodeties, and the plentie. Though Suffolke be more highlie comended of some wherewith I am not yet aquaynted. But this shire seemeth to me to deserve the title of the Engishe Goshen, the fattest of lande Comparable to Palestina, that flowed with milke and hunnye.

... ... the Hundreds of Vttlesforde, Chelmsforde, Clauerings, and those parties are reasonable apt for corne, and especialle Vttlesforde hundred, the rest are here and there much interlaced with wooded and rugged groundes.

... ... There is also nere Hatfield Broadokes a chase called Hatfield chace, a grounde well replenished with fallow deer"

John Norden (Map Maker) "Description of Essex" 1594

Some 230000 years ago in the third ice age known as the Riss Glaciation, immense deposits of boulder clay were forced up from the North Sea and deposited extensively over eastern England upon the existing base of chalk. This was then followed by a warm period lasting until 100000 BC when Europe underwent the last Great Ice Age, yielding a cover of loess which infiltrated into the clay top soil and eventually resulted in the conditions conducive to heavy forestation. In Essex these forests extended from Forest Gate on the outskirts of London in the south, up to the Suffolk border and across to the north-eastern corner of the county. Thus Essex was divided geographically - boulder clay to the northwest, London clay to the south, sand and gravel through the Blackwater estuary and marsh and peat to the east and along the north bank of the Thames. Locally this sheet of clay runs unbroken from Hatfield Forest through to Hatfield Broad Oak, the Easters, the Rodings and back through Matching, although at Hatfield Heath a seam of loam runs around the Heath which gave rise to its natural open space. The dense forest took some 4500 years to establish, and traces of which remain in the Essex forests we know today at Hainault, Epping, Waltham, Writtle, Wintry, Kingswood and our own Hatfield Forest.

The first inhabitants of Essex were probably the Palaeolithic who were then succeeded by the Mesolithic people some 6000 years ago, no evidence, however, of their presence has been found in the district. The humans who made

A History of Hatfield Heath

the first identifiable and hence significant impact in this region were the Neolithic people and proof of their habitation has been discovered at Pierce Williams where earthworks, flat tools and crude pottery have been found. Neolithic man was primarily a hunter and nomadic in nature, but some 4500 years ago it appears they took up cultivation of crops and kept livestock, creating open areas or utilising the natural open spaces such as the Heath. Thus began the slow but gradual destruction of the huge forest areas of Essex, which would continue over the course of the next 4000 years.

During the Bronze age this part of Essex was sparsely populated, although at Matching Barns, on Lord Rookwood's property, an important hoard of Bronze Age relics were found in 1893 which are now exhibited in the Colchester's Castle Museum. The forests did not themselves gain a measure of habitation until the Iron Age and even then settlements were relatively few, but traces of enclosures have been discovered at Portingbury Hills in the Forest and at Wallbury overlooking the river Stort.

In the centuries leading up to the Roman occupation in 54 B.C., agriculture, and in particular corn growing, was the main economic activity in Essex as it was to be for centuries to come. The Essex tribe of Celts, the Trinovantes, provided corn for Caesar's troops as a type of protection payment. The Trinovantes were based in Colchester and their rival tribe of Catvelluni came from St Albans, they being divided by the rivers Stort and Lea. About A.D. 41, however, Cunobelin the great Catvellunin leader occupied Essex and built his capital at Colonia near Colchester. The Romans in their second permanent occupation would have used the fortress at Wallbury as a means of keeping peace between these tribes. Despite their initial hostility the indigenous Britons finally settled down to Roman rule and its way of life and over the next 400 years the country's infrastructure underwent much change and beneficial improvement. There are some examples of Roman influence in the area including a temple at Harlow and some brickwork found in both Hallingbury churches as well as evidence of a Roman village around the Goose Lane area, uncovered when the M11 was under construction. Later, in 1999 on the Stonehall Farm some Roman burial artifacts were discovered. Additionally the Romans developed Stane Street connecting Braughing to Colchester although the original route was possibly much earlier.

After years of hostile incursions the Anglo Saxons finally settled in East Anglia in A.D. 526 and returned the country to its rural traditions bringing a revolution in agriculture in this part of the country. The Saxons were the principal exponents of the heavy plough and attached great importance to

Early History

the fields, particularly the strip system, which avoided the plough having to turn many times, although this method was by no means predominant in West Essex. Roads were therefore required to go round fields, hence the characteristic of Essex winding ways.

Around A.D. 597 King Ethelbert of Kent had much influence in Essex and did much good work for the population. The Saxon system brought about a complex agricultural society and although early settlements tended to be of a nomadic nature they eventually were broken up into smaller static manorial units. After the royal estates and the estates of the Thanes, the manorial system was the Saxon's method of control and administration as it also enforced local laws and the Lord of the Manor's rights. When the Saxon King Erkenwin ruled Essex the feudal system brought about the enclosure of much woodland and heath in West and North Essex, and at Mascallsbury, White Roothing evidence of a very old Saxon homestead has been located.

In A.D. 634 Christianity began to spread under Oswald. Cedd established a church at Bradwell on the Essex coast around A.D. 663 then Sebert became the first Christian King of Essex. In A.D. 664 the Great Abbey at Barking was founded by Earenwald. The occupation of Essex by the Saxons lasted 500 years but was not continuous. The east of England was ravaged by Danish invaders who won great battles at Maldon in A.D. 991, where brave Byrhtnoth the Ealdorman of Essex was slain, and again at Ashington in A.D. 1016. The Saxons of Essex then felt the harshness of King Canute's rule, although he did much to reconcile the Saxon and the Dane. Only when the surviving Saxon heir Edward (The Confessor) was crowned in A.D. 1042 did a Saxon kingdom prevail for another 24 years.

The name of Hatfield derives from the Saxon "Hatfeilda" meaning open ground (a clearing in the forest) and "Heath"- uncultivated open ground, most of this part of Essex at this time being wooded. The Heath itself would have been regarded as "Manorial Waste" and the whole Parish was designated as part of the Harlow half-hundred, there being twenty hundreds in Essex. Hatfield had the appendage Regis as the area was owned by the King Edward the Confessor, the title passing into the hands of the wealthy and powerful Godwin family through marriage. The area was excellent hunting country and was used by Harold Godwin before he became King Harold II in 1066. A Saxon meeting cross, and later a church was built at Hatfield Regis and the town became a place of some importance with a variety of shops and trades, some peculiar to this region. There were in fact only two towns in Essex of any size, Colchester in the north and Maldon in the east and therefore the west of the County was served by such as Hatfield Broad Oak.

A History of Hatfield Heath

There were ten medieval manors within the parish of Hatfield Regis, some originally being only a tenement of the great Manor of Hatfield. Of these only parts of the original Old Town building (Hatfield Bury) still survives. Within the present parish of Hatfield Heath were the moated Lea Hall (John de la Lee and Peter of Haslingfield) Down Hall (la Doune Manor) and Ries (Geoffrey de Mandeville and Robert Gernon). In Hatfield Regis were Little Barrington (Eustace Barrington) rebuilt in the 16th century and still in excellent condition, Bonnington (William Bollington), Broomshawbury (Richard de Brunesho), and Pierce Williams (Peter son of Williams) all rebuilt in the 19th century. The manors of Matching Barns and Brent Hall are no longer with us, indeed very little of the fabric of Saxon England is still evident today.

Upon the death of Harold in 1066 the estate of Hatfield Regis passed to William I (The Conqueror) who used the forest for his passion of hunting. He did however give a portion of the tithes to his half sister's husband Alberic De Vere for service during the battle of Hastings and it was de Vere's grandson, the first Earl of Oxford, who in 1135 founded the Priory of Hatfield Regis for the Benedictine order of St Melanius of Rennes. The Manor itself was granted to Robert de Gernon who took the title of Lord Mountfitchet and it was his authority that enabled the permanent establishment of the early Priory.

The Priory would have played an important part in the life of Hatfield both as landowner, employer, builder, teacher and to render assistance to the poor and aged. The town carried a Sunday market from A.D. 1200 and a Saturday market was started 18 years later. In addition to its manors the parish supported some large messuages (farms). These included Ongars, adjacent to the Heath, Shrubbs (Robert Shrowes bailiff to Hatfield Manor) recorded from 1297, Lankesters, (owned by John De Lancaster), Parvills, (Hugo De Pereville) formerly a free tenement of the manor of Matching Hall, Gladwyns (John de Gladewyne), Skringills, recorded as Corringales from 1217 and Branktrees (Adam Braintree), later owned by the Joscelyns of Hyde Hall. Most of their lands were within the present parish of Hatfield Heath although at this time a homestead at Clipped Hedge is believed to be the only building actually situated on the Heath. Thus the area was to prosper through its manors, farms, hamlets, greens and common land.

Norman law held that no land should be lordless and no county bears the imprint of their rule more than Essex. They reinforced the Saxon manorial system, making everyone responsible to their Lord, and the Lord's allegiance was to his King. In Hatfield a high proportion of its inhabitants were 5th, 6th and 7th class villeins, cotters, and akermani (bonded tenants), the fourth class being freemen. The Lord of the Manor exercised control through his seneschal (steward) and his bailiffs. The Normans ran the country very much as a military and feudal operation, but built many fine churches and abbeys in Essex and did not seem to find this piety incompatible with their harsh methods of subjugation.

In 1086 the population of the parish of Hatfield Regis, living in 114 homes, was the 9th largest in Essex with some 25 hides under cultivation. Over the next two centuries more land and forest was converted to agriculture. Elm disease, however, was also responsible for the contraction of Essex forests. By this time the kings tended to employ professional hunters to meet the needs of their table. At Christmas in 1251 the Court of Henry III ate 430 red deer, 200 fallow deer, 200 roe deer, 200 wild swine and an assortment of swans, hares, cranes and other beasts and birds, many coming from his forest at Hatfield. He was known to have visited Hatfield Regis on the 29th August 1229.

In 1140 Stephen gave the tithes of Hatfield to Geoffrey De Mandeville but he was soon to be out of favour and the title passed to Richard De Lucy, then in 1157 to Walter De Hatfield. In 1179 the titles were acquired by Pair De Rochford and then in 1200 by Guy De Poscene. In 1214 they became the responsibility of the Priory.

Since 1136 Hatfield Regis had become known as Hatfield Broad Oak after the great oak 'on the road west to the Mill'. The Mill lay west of Hatfield Broad Oak (where Bleak House in now situated) therefore it appears that the Great Oak was situated in or near Hatfield Heath. There is a reference in 1628 to the Great Oak of Hatfield Heath being sold for £5. There were, however, other giant oaks in the area, notably the famous Doodle Oak in the forest near to Stane Street, which dated from around A.D. 950. It was cut down in 1807 although parts remained until 1924, giving it an existence of nearly 1000 years. Apart from the windmill mentioned above which was recorded as being situated in 'Mill Field', there were also two other mills recorded in medieval times, one at Monk's Field NE of Broad Oak and one to the east of Hatfield Heath.

Edward III granted estates at Hatfield to William De Cassinham in A.D. 1217. From A.D.1238 to 1306 it passed to the Bruce family who had considerable estates in Chester and in Essex. Isabella de Bruce had a residence at Broomshawbury but it was her grandson Robert who lost these possessions upon his Scottish rebellion in 1314. The tithes were then acquired by the

A History of Hatfield Heath

military earls of de Bohun until 1421 and the Stafford family until 1547. This unfortunate family lost their heads as well as their property when they fell out with King Henry VIII who favoured the infamous Lord Rich, founder of Felsted School. In 1612 the Rich family sold its interest in the forest to the Barringtons who already owned the Priory buildings.

The 13th and 14th centuries saw the Priory grow in wealth and power. The traveller approaching Hatfield Broad Oak was presented with the spectacular sight of the two towers appearing above Langbridge Street (Feathers Hill) as they sought refuge, hospitality and spiritual counsel within its walls. Robert Taper, a wealthy noble, and his wife Millicent gave part of the Down estate to the Priory as well as land in Hatfield Regis. It was mainly due to the Tapers and one John de Bledawe and his wife Alice that the Priory was rebuilt and beautified in the first quarter of the Fourteenth Century. The Priory was, however, not without its problems. A fire destroyed part of the church in 1230. The appointment of a new Prior in 1257 by the Abbot of Rennes was disputed by the monks and the Bishop of London and lasted many years being taken to the Pope for his arbitration. By 1378 the vicar and parishioners were involved in disputes with the Priory over various matters and these was bought to a head with England's war with France when the local citizens viewed the Priory as being foreign property. They attacked the buildings and ejected the monks. As a consequence King Richard II ordered a wall to be built between the parish and monastic churches and this wall survives as the east wall of the present parish church. The Priory did however have some distinguished Priors, in 1400 John Cock was promoted to Papal Chaplain and in 1423 John Lydgate the prolific poet and academic was elected Prior. About 1386 extensive new building work had been undertaken in both parish and monastic churches and the building would then have resembled a small cathedral.

During the 12th, 13th and the first half of the 14th century life in an Essex village had mixed blessings. The poor 'paid' rent for their land mainly with tasks performed for their masters such as ploughing, reaping and woodcutting. The signing of the Magna Carta in 1215, which included the signature of local Baron Robert de Vere 3rd Earl of Oxford, had done little to help their plight, they could not marry without permission of their lord nor move outside the manor, however within these restrictions most enjoyed a secure and well ordered life. To this day the soil of the Heath is owned by the Lord of the Manor and there are some houses still with grants of Rights of Common to graze, collect wood and hunt rabbits! Farming in this area was making large strides in innovation and husbandry; villages were self-supporting with

Early History

artisans available for their needs and for repairs. Local responsibilities would have included pressed labour for road maintenance, but the repair of bridges was the duty of farmers and estates, i.e. the Chelmsford Road crossing of Pincey Brook, Stone Bridge, being cared for by Hill and Friars farms and that of the Down crossing, built in 1322, being cared for by the Down estate. Discipline was kept through the Manor Courts (titheings). Markets and Fairs in the district were numerous and gave people a chance to sell as well as buy articles not available in the villages. Church festivals also gave the poor a break from the humdrum of their every day lives and brought a small amount of colour to their otherwise dull existence. By 1327 Hatfield Broad Oak ranked 6th in terms of County taxpayers. Hatfield Heath peasants, at this time, were not often too bothered by their somewhat remote masters, fearing more the plague, lawlessness and economic deprivation.

By the middle of the 14th century the manorial system was showing signs of breaking up, the parish by now being the principle unit of local administration. The Black Death of 1348 saw some Essex villages lose over half their population and in some cases whole families were wiped out, although the younger generation tended to survive and inherit. At the hamlet of Morrells Roding (Cammas Hall) the plague killed everyone living there. In 1381 in the Peasant's Revolt, the villeins of Essex under Jack Straw joined those of Kent to demand their freedom. After initial appeasement it was ruthlessly crushed and the leaders executed. This insurrection helped undermine a system which had been the core of ordinary people's lives for more than 600 years. Much of the land in the Hatfields had been enclosed by the mid 15th Century as the tenants consolidated their own strips (free virgates). A virgate being about 30 acres. The Manors, therefore, were experiencing difficulties in enforcing their villeins and cotters work services, so by the 16th century the link between landlord and tenant had become mainly a cash one. It was at the time of the 1381 riots that many manorial rolls were taken and destroyed. Records before then in Essex are hard to find although Broad Oak kept some of the oldest in Essex. England did manage to retain an efficient central government, which was improved in 1430 when the first members from the Shires were returned to Parliament by elections. Ultimately the growth in trade and money was the main cause in undermining the old manorial system.

The Wars of the Roses brought a check to this growth and although there was no strife in Essex, the De Bohun family lost their Hatfield estates to the Lancastrian cause in 1461.

A major change came to the people of Essex, and to Hatfield Broad Oak in particular, when in 1536 Henry V111 was in dispute with Rome and on 8th

A History of Hatfield Heath

July passed an Act dissolving the Monasteries. The Priory then came under the patronage of Barking Abbey until 1538 when the Priory's fabric was destroyed, although by this time only 4 monks remained in the local community. The estates of the Priory were then assessed by a commission under Sir John Seyntcher and were sold for the benefit of King Henry. Although some remains of the Priory were evident in 1766 nothing now stands above ground. The Norman church, however, was left untouched and was bequeathed to the patronage of Trinity College Cambridge. The domestic buildings passed to one Thomas Nokes and in 1564 to Thomas Barrington. The Priory's land at Down was sold to William Beuers, Walter Farre and William Glasscock. The Barrington family were to consolidate their position locally by acquiring the Manors at Matching Barns, Brent Hall and later, Pierce Williams and Bollingtons as well as Lancasters farm. The manors of Lea Hall and Ryes in the second half of the 15th Century were the homes of the prominent Yorkist lawyer Sir Thomas Unwick and in the 16th Century were owned by the influential Frank family. This family sold Lea Hall, however, to John Munford in 1612.

On religious matters, at this time, much of Essex was hostile to Rome partly through the influence of the reformist preachers, consequently many suffered under the religious strictures of the time. Protestants under Mary Tudor and then Catholics under Queen Elizabeth I were both, in their turn, penalised for adhering to their religious beliefs. Despite these tribulations a school for the gentry's children was opened in Broad Oak in 1564. Although schooling for children had been available from the Guild's Chantry school by 1450 no major attempt at tuition for the poor was made until 1686. Another peculiarity at this time was the levy of a special poll tax by the parish on all adults of Hatfield Broad Oak. Despite all these social and political upheavals the parish of Broad Oak, patronised by one of the oldest guilds in Essex, (founded in 1363,) was still able to support a population of over 1000 by 1546.

There was a great movement in house building in Essex in the 2nd half of the 16th century and in 1565 the original Barrington Hall near the forest was demolished and the current farmhouse built. The Barringtons could trace their history back to Ethelred and held the title of "Woodward". As protectors of Hatfield Forest, they held land at Hatfield Regis in 1130 and their names appeared on parliamentary rolls from 1330. From the 17th century the Barringtons also had interests in the West Indies. The Broad Oak annual St James fair on 25th July was moved in 1609 with much protest to Thremhall Green, south of Stane Street, and this brought about a dispute between the Morleys of Hallingbury Place, the Leventhorpes and the

Early History

Barringtons over fair rights and resulted in confrontation and violence on fair days. The dispute was finally settled in court with the Barringtons winning, and in 1621 the fair was moved back to Broad Oak, however it was subsequently moved to Hatfield Heath in 1660 and had faded away by 1860.

The dissolution of the monasteries meant that one means of caring for the poor and elderly had ceased to exist, and in 1597 and 1601 Parliament found it necessary to pass statutes making churchwardens responsible for these needs. The vestry system was therefore instituted which would deal with local affairs for some 350 years until the passing of the Poor Law Act in 1834. The vestry consisted of two churchwardens, one appointed by the parish church and one by the rate payers who were mainly the gentry and the landowners or landholders of the parish. In addition there was the office of Constable responsible for civil order, two Surveyors responsible for roads and infrastructure of the parish, usually 'pressed' into service on a rota basis, and of most importance, Overseers of the Poor, again pressed into the job on a similar rota basis. At Hatfield Broad Oak there was one Overseer of the Poor for each four quarters, reduced from the original eight titheings, and these were named as - The Town, Woodroe, Bromsend and the Heath. Thus all property owners in Hatfield Heath, mainly farmers, male and female (no discrimination), took their turn in this onerous task in rotation, i.e. Gladwyns one year, Ongars the next, then Parvilles etc. This involved assessing the needs of the poor and elderly, calculating a rate based on the rental value of land and levying this rate, usually in six months periods, and then its collection and distribution. At the end of his term the Overseer would present his accounts to the magistrate and, with luck, be signed off for perhaps another 10-12 years.

The 16th and 17th century saw the decline of Hatfield Broad Oak as a major town in the area. The dissolution of the Priory, the loss of the fair and the centralisation of the Barrington Estate outside the town all led to its demise. Earlier the Black Death had most certainly ravaged the town and in 1603 there was a bad outbreak of the plague in Essex which would have affected a community such Hatfield Broad Oak. Houses were left in a state of disrepair and some fell down. This contrasted with the fortunes of Hatfield Heath recorded as a hamlet in 1442, with just fourteen homesteads, but by the 17th Century it had become a main area of settlement. Its position on the main thoroughfares between Epping, Dunmow, Chelmsford, Bishop's Stortford and Braintree brought about the carrier trade which added to the economy of the village.

A History of Hatfield Heath

The outbreak of the Civil War saw Essex solid for Parliament, with the Earl of Warwick and Sir Thomas Barrington strong supporters for Parliament's cause. Sir Thomas's father Sir Francis Barrington, related by marriage to Oliver Cromwell, had served the Country nobly under both James I and Charles I. In spite of this Charles had him thrown into prison because of his refusal to make a loan of ship money to the King and he died as a the result of his incarceration. Sir Thomas Barrington kept detailed diaries of his parliamentary career and these are deposited in the British Museum and form an important part of the history of the time. Sir Thomas's son Sir John Barrington and grandson Sir Charles Barrington also represented this area in Parliament. The everyday life of the inhabitants of Hatfield Heath was little affected by the war.

A new dimension to the spiritual and the social life of Hatfield Heath was added in 1662 when the Rev. John Warren refused to accept the Act of Uniformity and the Book of Common Prayer and was deprived of his living. This living was in fact badly paid, for although Hatfield Broad Oak was a large parish, it was so poorly endowed that Trinity College Cambridge, the patrons, refused for some time to present an incumbent. Rev. Warren moved to Hatfield Heath and after receiving a licence in 1672 started religious meetings in the village. This was held at the house of Ann Parker, which was possibly situated in the west of the Heath, for in 1680 Lady Dorothy Barrington and others were fined 'for attending a conventicle' at the home of Ann Parker. In 1689 the Tolerance Act was passed and the non-conformists Presbyterian Church was officially established. An application to worship in a converted house was passed in 1706 and a barn was used from 1724. It soon became dilapidated and therefore in 1726 the freehold of the present site was obtained and a new meeting house built, to which, in 1730 a manse was added. The congregation about this time was some 300 worshippers with the strong support of local farmers. After the initial growth of non-conformity in East Anglia in the later part of the 17th Century when several training colleges at Cambridge served this area well, many of these churches then declined in the early part of the 18th century. This does not though appear to be the case in Hatfield Heath.

By 1662 there were 162 properties in the parish, but most dwellings in this period were very humble, even for the better off farm worker. The house would have comprised a middle room with hearth and bold central chimney stack with a small parlour on one side and the stairs to the bedrooms on the other. The master bedroom would have been in the middle with the daughters' bedroom over the parlour and the sons' bedroom on the opposite side

Early History

over the stair well. On the Heath the only relief from a long day's work on the farm would have been the occasional fair, the religious festivals, the alehouses and from 1662, the social offering of a non-conformist meeting group. The cloth industry provided a secondary income for the poor for there were weaving centres in Dunmow, Braintree and Harlow as well as a silk industry in Hatfield Broad Oak. It required 10 spinners to keep a weaver going and this gave a supplementary income to the poor families where the work could be undertaken by the wife, daughter and grandmother in their own home. The plague of 1665 was, however, a hindrance to growth and hit Essex hard with 665 people dying in Braintree alone.

Due to a mistaken instruction the old priory domestic buildings were pulled down in 1710 while Sir Charles Barrington was away. A new Barrington Hall was built to the north of Hatfield Park in 1740 by John Barrington Shales, the new Lord of the Manor. At this time the agriculture industry was in recession and this was felt in the Hatfields. The population was some 800 of which only 92 were ratepayers and only 20% were artisans and shopkeepers. In 1722 Defoe visited the parish and recorded 'of much good husbandry and malt, but only three ale houses and mean ones at that, no great thoroughfare and little trade'. After 1740, however, there was a rise in the fortunes of Essex farmers, who were some of the most enterprising in the whole country growing barley for malt and giving a good deal of time in using new machinery and improved drainage and cultivation. The average size of a farm in the Hatfields in the later part of the 18th Century was around 200 acres. Within the parish there were two windmills recorded at this time, one at the Down Hall estate, owned by 'widow' Joscelyn (no record after 1841), the other at Holsted Hill on the road to Broad Oak which was destroyed by the great storm of 1881. It is believed that the Down windmill was later re-erected on the south side of the lane to Parvilles and the miller was Ephraim Davey who later owned the mill built on the Heath. The opening of the Stour navigation in 1705, the Stort in 1769 and the Chelmer and Blackwater in 1797 and the turnpikes to Norwich and Colchester together with general improvements in roads, all helped create a prosperity which filtered down to the poor who were better off than ever before, although only the gentry were sufficiently wealthy to be mobile and to come and go in the district. At this time 3 out of every 5 people living on the Heath were born there.

During the 18th century many wealthy families began moving into Essex and built their grand houses, although they mainly concerned themselves with national matters rather than local administration. Mathew Prior poet and diplomat, responsible for writing the treaty of Utrecht, spent his last years at

A History of Hatfield Heath

Down under the patronage of Robert Harley, Earl of Oxford. By 1777 houses were ringing the Heath and three alehouses and inns were established. The Stag (originally called the Horseshoes then the Bald Stag), the White Horse and the Bell (recorded in 1769 but with no trace from 1782). The White Hart at Shrubbs seems also to have disappeared by 1769. Later the Beer Act of 1830 allowed any householder to become a beer retailer upon payment of two guineas to the Excise authority and this led to an expansion of alehouses, (the Old Stag, the Red Cow and the Brewery Tap). However by 1869 the sale of alcohol was brought under firmer control by the local Magistrates and most of these old alehouses closed, or as in the case of the Waggon & Horses converted to recognised inns. The Fox & Hounds was built about this time by the Bishop's Stortford brewers Hawkes & Co. who owned many local inns. Later these were all sold to the Benskins Company of Watford. A very early school opened on the Heath around 1840 and was run by a shoemaker and his wife. Shoemakers being artisans and not tied to landowners, as was the case with farm workers, were then considered to be the champions of the poor. In 1845 three shoemakers were recorded on Hatfield Heath; William Dennis, Steven Nash and James Dewbrey.

The rise of agriculture was balanced by a decline in the fortune of the cloth trade, although the silk industry prospered in Hatfield Broad Oak run by one John Gobert. The Peninsular war, the loss of the American Colonies and then the Napoleonic wars destroyed the weaving industry and the poorer families of the Hatfields lost a valuable supplement to their income. This is shown in the Broad Oak vestry records where in 1720 the Hatfield Heath quarter showed a requirement for the poor of £215 and in 1776 £546, by 1785 it was £748, then in 1803 £1,140, rising to £2,503 by 1813. The workhouse in Broad Oak had between 6 and 10 inhabitants in 1734; this had risen to 18 by 1775 but it was closed in 1836 when it became part of the Dunmow Union. Penalties for those who transgressed were very harsh. James Drake of Sawbridgeworth was stopped at Hatfield Heath on 26th April 1843 and found with 28 stolen fowls in his cart. At Chelmsford Court two months later he was sentenced to be transported to Australia for 15 years. Despite the poverty prevailing, the Town was able to hold its annual Lamb Fair on the 5th August for many years. However, by 1830 even this event had ceased. In 1798 there was great fear in East Anglia of a Dutch invasion and New Volunteer Companies staffed by local men were set up at Hallingbury Place (The Houblons) and at Hatfield Park (The Barringtons).

By the end of the 18th century agriculture was again in decline and the Saturday market had closed. This recession led to great discontent for some

Early History

73% of adult males in the parish were employed as farm workers. In 1800 there were food riots and in 1830 at Sheering, a minor rebellion (the Swing riots) led by one Capt. Swift over the use of the new threshing machines. As a result of their frustration the poor took to arson as a means of attacking their masters. In Essex this action became known as `Horrid Lights' and was a feature of this part of the County for several years. In December 1843, at Chelmsford, Michael Challis, of Hatfield Broad Oak, was sentenced to be transported for setting fire to a farm at Campions, Harlow. There were also many accidental fires in the district later in this century. Some were serious, such as the fires at Gladwyns in 1865, at Henry Sullin's maltings on the Broad Oak Road in 1882 and in 1887 at Mr Cooper's field next to the brewery. Local farmers were to suffer further in 1844 when a severe storm with huge hailstones cut a 3/4 mile swathe from Broad Oak through the Heath and into Sheering damaging buildings and crops on its way. In 1700 there had been 40 farms in Hatfield Heath, some of course which were small, but by 1800 these had reduced to 22, of which Matching Barns was the largest covering 360 acres and having 11 employees, Friars/Gt. Heath - 340 acres and employing 13, Corringales - 200 acres with 7 men and Lea Hall -164 acres and 6 workers. Gladwins - 120 acres 7 men and Shrubbs -147 acres 7 men were the other farms of any size. By 1875, however, only 13 farms remained. The parish of Broad Oak covered some 8781 acres and there was in Hatfield Heath at this time 1731 acres under cultivation, with 109 acres of common land in the parish of which the Heath common (34 acres) was the largest. The commons of Bentley and Muchfield bordering each side of Friars Lane as well as Hart and Jackson Commons had been under cultivation for many centuries and until 1841 retained some evidence of the strip system. Most local farms were worked by tenant farmers who not only paid a rent to the landlord, but also rates and a tithe rent to the Church. Parvilles farm of 71 acres paid an annual rent of £100, rates of £5-7s-3d and a tithe of £19-16s-9d. Details of the parish were by now much more clearly documented by the National Census, the first being in 1801 and the first for the Heath, as a separate parish, taken in 1881. In addition Essex has excellent tithe maps dating from 1838. Tithes were the method in which the church imposed taxes in order to maintain their funds. These maps and its key gave the location of every field and homestead, even down to the kitchen size hoppets, as well as its cultivation, its owner and its occupier. Tithes were abolished in 1936.

The Barrington Line ended in 1832 with the death of Sir Fitzwilliam Barrington and the Lord of the Manor's title passed through the female line to William Selby Lowndes. A great sale of the Barrington properties in Hatfield Heath (The South Division) occurred on 16th June 1841 after the

A History of Hatfield Heath

Manor was acquired by GA Lowndes from Thomas Lowndes. The farms at Lancasters, Manwood, Blocks, Matching Barns, and Stonehall were acquired by the Selwin-Ibbertson estate at Down. Shortly after in 1853 the St Bartholomew Hospital Trust sold their farms at Gt. Heath and Lt. Heath and in 1854 Parvilles, tenanted by Peter Sullins, also became part of the Down estate. About this time the estates at Hallingbury, which included parts of the forest, were purchased by the Houblon family who were Flemish immigrants and founders of the Bank of England. John Houblon, by an Act of Parliament of 1857, and at considerable expense to himself, enclosed the Forest and built a lake and the Shell House. Although his relationship with the Barringtons did involve much litigation it was far more amicable than had been the case with the Rich and Morley families where, but for the smart intervention of the vicar of Hatfield, Lord Morley would have grabbed the Forest lands for himself.

As well as these influential families there were other wealthy land owners living in Hatfield Heath in the 19th century and these include Loftus Arkwright and then Horace Broke a barrister and his wife Isobel both of Gladwyns, Sir Henry Selwin-Ibbertson, later Lord Rookwood of Down Hall, a distinguished M.P. and Government Minister representing several Essex Constituencies from 1865 to 1892 and his wife Eden, the Rev. Payne, a retired cleric, William Dore J.P. and Miss Sara Wiseman all of Hatfield Heath Grange. These families were great benefactors to the Heath and the Brokes were to be steadfast servants of Holy Trinity when it was finally built and for many years after. Further benefactors to the village and its churches, during the 19th Century, included the Poole family of Matching Hall and later Oaklands, the Lowndes from Barrington Hall, the Houblons of Hallingbury Place who owned considerable lands around the Heath, the Matthews of Housham Hall and of Campions, Barnard Matthews of Gibsons, the Hockley families and Miss Sarah Chamberlayne of Ryes who apart from other gifts also provided a charitable trust for the elderly of several local villages.

In February 1862 a Hatfield Heath butcher, James Robinson died suddenly in his 45th year. He was reputed to be the largest man in Essex and Hertfordshire and perhaps all England, for he weighed 36 stone with a girth of 70 inches. His butchers business was continued after his death by Thomas Cooper. The American author Francis Marion Crawford stayed at Hatfield Broad Oak in about 1878 as a student under the care of the Vicar the Rev George Burns. He later wrote a novel which reflected his experiences whilst living in the area called *"Tales from a lonely Parish'."* At this time too Miss Harriet Bolton Barlow, who was a well-known decorator of Royal Doulton ware, lived on the Heath. Some of her work is on show in the Bishop's Stortford Local History Museum.

Early History

After 1840 the agriculture industry was once again flourishing in Essex and this created more local wealth. The Lea and Stort Navigation had assisted in establishing malt houses along their banks and in addition some local farmers including Peter Sullins and Israel Mann not only grew barley but also produced malt and brewed their own beer. Some farms such as Friars were even operating their own brew houses. All over Great Britain there was a change in the economic climate. The Victorians were beginning to sing the praises of work, skill, enterprise and industrial success as shown by the Great Exhibition of 1851 and in the expansion of overseas trade. The repeal of the Corn Law of 1846 was to benefit agriculture through free trade for the next 30 years. The old poor laws and vestry system were replaced in 1834 by a new Poor Law where parishes were grouped into administrative unions with boards of governors (early Quango's ?) with Hatfield Broad Oak, including the Heath, becoming part of the Dunmow Union. A County Constabulary was formed in 1840 under the long serving Capt. McHardy and other social improvements were being made at this time. Mr Speller, for years, ran his donkey and cart service called the 'Hatfield Express' to Broad Oak and a coach service to London ran from the Heath in 1818 and to Bishop's Stortford from 1838. The Saffron Walden bank Gibson, Tuke and Gibson opened branches in Bishop's Stortford and Sawbridgeworth in 1826, these Banks being incorporated into Barclay's Bank in 1896. A postal service was started in Hatfield Heath from 1832 and the first Reform Act was passed in that same year. The North Eastern Railway opened from Sawbridgeworth in 1842 and the Takeley branch line opened in 1869. These enterprises enabled the poor to travel long distances and greatly improved communications.

The Parish Church of Hatfield Heath was built in 1859 on land given by the Lord of the Manor Alan Lowndes and with immense help from the mother church of St. Mary's Hatfield Broad Oak. Thus in the following year, 1860, Hatfield Heath became a separate ecclesiastical parish. Under the long serving minister the Rev. Cornelius Berry the chapel on the Chelmsford Road was enlarged in 1830 and in 1857 the British School built as a day school for pupils of all denominations at a charge of 2p per week, 1p if you were very poor. Attendance in 1857 was 113 children. An earlier Congregational school had been run from the manse from 1765 and this Church, under Cornelius Berry enjoyed congregations on Sundays of 400+ with a very large membership. A Dame School was believed to have started in 1840 in the care of James Dewbrey shoemaker and his wife. Then in 1856 a thatched cottage, near the windmill to the south of the Heath, became the National School. A makeshift corrugated tin hut opposite Holy Trinity was erected and used temporarily before the church authorities at Holy Trinity built, in 1863, a new school and

A History of Hatfield Heath

teacher's house on the Heath. This old school is now known as the Institute. In 1875 the new Congregational Church was built on the Chelmsford Road and designed to seat over 450 persons. Another local benefit was created in 1867 when the old silk mill at Hatfield Broad Oak was converted into a cottage hospital with 4 beds and later, in 1892, was enlarged with funds provided by Lord and Lady Rookwood. In 1899 the name of the hospital was changed to Eden in memory of Lady Rookwood. Medical care for the poor had always been provided on a casual basis but from 1872 the Union was paying doctors an annual retainer to assist those who could not afford fees.

Hatfield Heath (and all Essex) was to suffer another agricultural recession by the mid 1870s when the development of the railways in America and steam navigation allowed the farmers of the mid-west to export their grain to Europe very cheaply. A Hatfield Broad Oak Agricultural Friendly Society was formed in 1870 led by the Millbank Brothers and Henry Sullins, but the writing was on the wall for only the most efficient farms could compete with these imports. On the Heath, where 40% of production was still wheat, from the 13 farms of any size in 1875, only 5 were producing corn by 1897. The number of farm workers in the Parish declined in the same period from 136 to 87. By 1900 only Mrs Pamphilon at Ongars was holding out as a grain producer. "Land has ceased to be either a profit or a pleasure," said Oscar Wilde in 1895. Some farmers emigrated to try their fortunes in Canada and new tenant farmers such as the Broads, the Padfields, the Sopers, the Gartons, the Scantleburys, the Lukies, the Gemmells, and the Andersons and later the Liddells moved in from Cornwall and from Scotland to try their luck at farming in East Anglia. Indeed the area around Chelmsford was often referred to as the `Scotch Colony'. The Hockley family, however, were from Essex stock with Daniel and John Hockley snr coming from Thaxted in 1869 to take over from David Surridge as tenant farmers at Friars. William Hutchin who farmed at Peggerells was, however, from a locally born family. Other Heath tenant farmers enduring the hardships of these times included Stephan Pamphilon - Lea Hall, Martha Eades - Corringales, Noah Griggs - Lt Heath, Daniel Brown - Gladwyns, Thos Hayden - Lancasters, Samuel Mumford, Frederick Cooper-Blocks, James Dixon - Ryes and Isaac Thorogood, of Great Heath farm. The population of the village declined from 700 in 1881 to 635 in 1891 and to 579 by 1901, with many sons going to the Metropolis to work in the new factories, and daughters going to far away places to work in service to the gentry. Despite this, the farm workers that were left were better off as demand for their labour was greater due to the drift to towns. A farm labourer of 1840 earned 8/- per week but by 1891 this had increased to 12/-. In addition the cost of living was very stable and purchasing power was far greater that 50 years before. At that rate of pay it must have felt very costly for one Heath resident a John Brown, hay carter, who on 29th June 1899 was find 15/- for driving while asleep at Sheering. This did not appear to be much of a deterrent as on 5th May 1900 P.C. Brown of Harlow stopped the defendant's cart as it apparently did not have a driver. Upon further investigation the constable found Mr Brown in the back of the cart under the hay with a young woman! He was fined 20/-. Life could be very hard for these carters with long hours and many accidents occurring. In 1863 James Clarke, employed by Noah Griggs of Little Heath farm fell under the cartwheels at Loughton and sustained serious injuries.

The people of Hatfield Heath were, at this time, finding new ways of earning a living. A windmill, called Merchaws Mill was built in 1841 on the south side of the Heath and originally owned by Ephraim Davey. Sidney Oliver was the owner at the turn of the century. In 1890 auxiliary steam power was added. It closed 1906 finally to be demolished in 1909 when owned by William Bowyer and Richard Martin Broad. In 1845 a brewery employing three people was started on the road to Gladwyns, probably by Peter Sullins a local farmer and landlord of the Cock. A John Burrett was a thatcher as well as running a coal and corn business from the Old Stag in 1845, and John Witham was also operating as a corn merchant and general carrier. Earlier Richard Searle was the village blacksmith; Richard Wentworth the wheelwright and one John Norris traded as a basketmaker. In 1861 William Vale, a blacksmith originally from Hallingbury, started a threshing business and in 1881 his son Walter Vale, who lived at Oak Lodge, was importing and selling agricultural machinery and employed 11 people, employees who previously would have been working on the land. This business was still operating in 1937. Aaron Hawkins, blacksmith of The Stag, continued the corn and coal business there as well as being in 1875 the Heath's first sub-postmaster. Mr Hawkins also gave charitable dinners to the poor of the Parish where sometimes 150-200 people would come to enjoy a free meal. In 1863 at the celebration of the Prince of Wales wedding to Princess Alexandra, Mr Stephen Pamphilon, Mr Thomas Poole and others provided a dinner at the new school (the Institute) for over 400 workers and their families who were waited on by local farmers and tradesmen. The landlord of the White Horse employed an ostler in an attempt to give an upmarket image to the coaching inn and he also worked as a local builder. At the Fox & Hounds an enterprising man from London ran a general dealership and carrier service. On the Stortford road, Peter Sullins built a Maltings and Brewery around 1860, which was later run by the Barnard family. In 1894 it was taken over by Charles Sutton Wardle and in 1898 by Gerald Bonham-Carter. The brewery finally closed in 1902 and

A History of Hatfield Heath

became a flourmill operated by the Edwards family. The position of the Heath was an important factor in these businesses, particularly the London hay carting trade and in addition the road system was improving. The old vestry system of pressed labour, working in many cases under a reluctant surveyor, had never been satisfactory, as over the centuries both local roads and bridges had fallen into disrepair. At the Essex Lent assizes in 1876 Henry Sullins and Aaron Hawkins petitioned the Authorities for non-repair of local roads. By now, however, professional contractors who had gained experience under Metcalf, Telford and Macadam were building and repairing thoroughfares with much greater skill.

Artisans were also affected by the agricultural demise and some drifted to the towns to work in factories but the Heath was still able to support ten shops, an unusually large number for a village. There were three butchers of whom two were farmers trying to supplement their reducing income from corn - Henry Bowyer and Thomas Cooper, the third being owned by James and Elizabeth Blatch. A George Isaac Harris, later postmaster, was a grocer. This shop had previously been run by Daniel Adams then by Sophie Howland. Other shops at this time were two bakers, one recorded as James Bacon, a sweet shop attended by Hannah Adams, a tobacconist, and a druggist run by a Miss Jane Perry and William Perry. In addition there was a smithy on the Stortford road run by William Perry and his son Charles Perry. John Witham of the Laurels was a corn and meal chandler who also operated a general stores from the Beehive. This establishment was later used by John Button for harness making, a business that previously had been owned by a George Brown. This business was continued by his son JJ Button until after the 2nd World War. Jane Clarke and Mary Stevens were dressmakers and Ben Biscoe was the local chimney sweep. On the south side of the Heath next to Davis Row, Thomas Mills, Stephen Nash and J Childs traded as shoemakers.

As the people of Hatfield Heath approached the end of the 19th century they were beginning to enjoy a more satisfying social life and, mainly through better funded schools and their own efforts, were educating themselves. Queen Victoria's Diamond Jubilee on 22nd June 1897 gave the country a feeling of confidence and was celebrated on the Heath with sports; a bonfire and a 'meat tea' organised by Messrs Bonham-Carter, Bowyer, Bretton, Poole and the Rev. Reeves Palmer. Three Duplex oil lamps were erected on the Heath to commemorate the Jubilee and the surplus from the festivities of £25 was spent on a new pump installed at Lilac Cottage on the Bishop's Stortford Road. Mr Percy Day who lived at Smarts Cottages for most of his life recalls as a young boy assisting Daniel Day to light these lamps on many a dark wet evening. The technique was for Daniel to climb the ladder first, then Percy would follow throwing a coat over Daniel's head and the lamp top as he struggled to strike a match against the winter wind. A Magazine Club for the benefit of villagers was run by the Hockley family for some 60 years from 1865 until it was amalgamated with the library in 1926. A working men's club called the 'Coffee and Reading Room' (Secretary Mr TW Brown) was started on the Heath in 1879 in a cottage "close to Mr Coopers" and was open from 6am to 10pm weekdays. Mr Cooper's butcher's shop was situated where the Countryman restaurant now trades. In the same year at the British School a Temperance Society started with 35 members. Later, in 1900, when the new Church School was built by local builder EH Hockley, a men's club and reading room was opened in the Institute and was run by an elected village committee. From 1884 Dixon's steam fair visited the Heath using a field next to the vicarage. Cycling was available to all and further helped to expand travel. In 1884 mainly due to the efforts of the vicar the Rev. AE Beavan a cricket club was formed, with Edwin Cates followed by CW Sharp and then Gerald Bonham-Carter as secretaries. A football club was also believed to have played its first match in 1894. The Bank Holiday Act of 1871 gave the public additional free time and in 1889 the county council, and local councils were elected for the first time by the new franchise which had been expanded in the last Reform Act of 1884. Thus it was on 17th December 1894 that the Hatfield Broad Oak Parish Council met for the first time under the Chairmanship of GA Lowndes. Heath representatives were Arthur Millbank and Henry Bowyer. A Parish magazine was started by the Rev. TW Ward on 1st September 1893 and the new Trinity Hall was erected a year later. Communications improved both by road and rail, a sub-post office was opened in 1875 and a telegraphic service in 1894. Postal deliveries were twice a day. Water was still supplied by a spring in the centre of the village through standpipes and from private wells, many of which were dug by a Mr Henry Ingold of Bishop's Stortford and Mr Deards of Harlow. The largest of these lies underneath the mill and former brewery on the Stortford Road and another can be found in the bar of the Stag. In May 1874 a grand christening of St Dunstan's Well in the village centre took place with Sir Henry & Lady Selwin-Ibbotson, Mr & Mrs Horace Broke and Col. Taylor MP in attendance. Finance for this well had been collected by Henry Sullins. There were some very fine examples of hand pumps within the parish including the one, which at present stands outside the Post Office. Four more oil lamps were erected by Thomas Barker around the Heath in 1901 paid for by public subscription and looked after by Daniel Day right up until the outbreak of the war in 1914. Other utilities, however, were not available until the second quarter of the 20th century, although Down Hall had a private gas supply in 1880.

The elderly residents of Hatfield Heath living in 1900 had experienced major changes during the reign of Queen Victoria. Standing at the threshold of a new era little could they have realised the great events and changes which would lead to the transformation of their lives and the lives of their children and grandchildren over the course of the coming century.

ESSEX.

PARTICULARS AND CONDITIONS OF SALE
OF VALUABLE

FREEHOLD ESTATES,

Containing, in the whole, upwards of

730 ACRES,

Situate in the Parishes of

HATFIELD REGIS, ALIAS HATFIELD BROAD OAK, MATCHING, GREAT CANFIELD, AND WHITE OR MORREL ROOTHING,

IN THE COUNTY OF ESSEX,

About 4 Miles from the Sawbridgeworth Station on the Eastern Counties' Railway, 7 from Dunmow, 12 from Epping, 7 from Bishop Stortford, 15 from Chelmsford, and 28 from London, and within 4 Miles of the navigable River Stort,

DIVIDED INTO CONVENIENT FARMS,

And let to highly respectable Tenants;

ALSO, SEVERAL CONVENIENT

FREEHOLD RESIDENCES,

BUSINESS PREMISES,

AND COTTAGES,

In the Town of HATFIELD BROAD OAK, and on HATFIELD HEATH,

The whole producing Rents, amounting to

£1,080 PER ANNUM;

ALSO,

VALUABLE RIGHTS OF PASTURAGE

On Hatfield Forest and on Hatfield Heath,

Available the greater part of the Year, (Land-Tax redeemed, except a small charge on Lot 1;)

WHICH WILL BE SOLD BY AUCTION,

BY MESSRS.

CRAWTER & DEATH

AT GARRAWAY'S COFFEE-HOUSE,

'CHANGE ALLEY, CORNHILL,

On WEDNESDAY, the 17th day of AUGUST, 1853, at ELEVEN o'Clock.

IN LOTS,

(Unless previously disposed of by Private Contract,) by direction of the Proprietor.

May be viewed by permission of the several Tenants; and Particulars, with Plans annexed, may be obtained of Messrs. TATHAM & PROCTER, Lincoln's Inn, London; at the Cock Inn, Hatfield Broad Oak; White Lion, Sawbridgeworth; George, Bishop Stortford; Saracen's Head, Dunmow; White Hart, Romford and Brentwood; Black Boy, Chelmsford; of Mr. Peter Sullens, Hatfield Broad Oak; and of Messrs. CRAWTER & DEATH, Auctioneers and Estate Agents, Cheshunt, Herts.

Notice of Sale of part of the Barrington Estate in 1853

SUMMARY.

Lot.	Names of Farms, &c.	Occupiers.	Quantities. A. R. P.	Annual Rents. £ s. d.
1	Carter's and Wise's Farms	William Griggs	187 1 30	145 0 0
2	Cottages and Gardens	James Cook or his Under-tenants	0 1 17	6 0 0
3	Cannon's Farm	Alfred Potter	41 1 26	45 0 0
4	Crab's Green Farm	John Surridge	99 1 37	120 0 0
5	Spurling's Farm	Peter Sullins	44 2 23	62 10 0
6	Anthony's Farm	Ditto	58 1 4	69 0 0
7	Meadow Land	Ditto	2 0 23	4 0 0
8	Two Cottages, Garden and Meadow	Wm. Stallibrass or his Under-tenants	0 2 29	7 5 0
9	Meadow Land	Peter Sullins	0 1 27	1 10 0
10	Cottage and Garden	John Staines	0 0 37	1 10 0
11	Meadow and Cottages	William Hammond and others	3 1 4	14 6 0
12	Cottage and Garden	John Rogers	0 0 37	2 10 0
13	Cottages	William Cracknell and John Bird	0 0 6	5 10 0
14	House and Garden	Ann Speller	0 0 24	14 0 0
15	Cottages, &c.	William Bird and Others	0 1 3	19 0 0
16	Ditto	John Skingle and Others	0 0 33	13 2 0
17	Ditto	John Read and Others	0 0 25	9 0 0
18	Cottage, Timber Yard, &c.	John Clark, &c.	0 0 32	6 0 0
19	Cottages, &c.	Luke Judd and Ephraim Martin	0 0 9	6 0 0
20	Houses, &c.	Edward Battle and Others	0 1 8	32 6 0
21	Cottages, &c.	William Porter and Others	0 1 9	11 8 0
22	House and Premises	George Parris	0 0 36	20 0 0
23	House, Shop & ditto	Thomas Potter and Peter Sullins	0 0 19	30 0 0
24	Houses and Premises	Isaac Bird and William Parker	0 0 15	16 10 0
25	House, Buildings and Premises	Joseph Riley, Esq.	0 0 19	14 0 0
26	Houses, ditto ditto	William Hudson and Others	0 0 30	23 0 0
27	Skinner's and Dyke's	Richard Parris	22 3 23	30 0 0
28	Great Heath Farm	Isaac Thorogood	77 2 21	98 0 0
29	Cottage and Garden	John Sapsford	0 1 12	2 10 0
30	Two ditto ditto	Peter Sullins and James Patmore	0 0 28	6 0 0
31	House, Buildings and Premises	James Robinson	0 1 25	13 18 0
32	Two Cottages and Gardens	Richard Baker and Moses Adams	0 0 14	6 6 0
33	Cottage and Garden	John Payne	0 0 25	2 15 0
34	Two ditto	Thomas Eaton and Charles Perry	0 1 8	6 0 0
35	Little Heath Farm	Noah Griggs	61 1 8	75 0 0
36	Parvill's Farm	Peter Sullins	71 0 25	100 0 0
37	Land	John Potter	56 2 28	38 0 0
		Total	732 0 18	£1076 16 0

Bill of Sale Summary of the Barrington Estate Great Sale in 1853

A History of Hatfield Heath

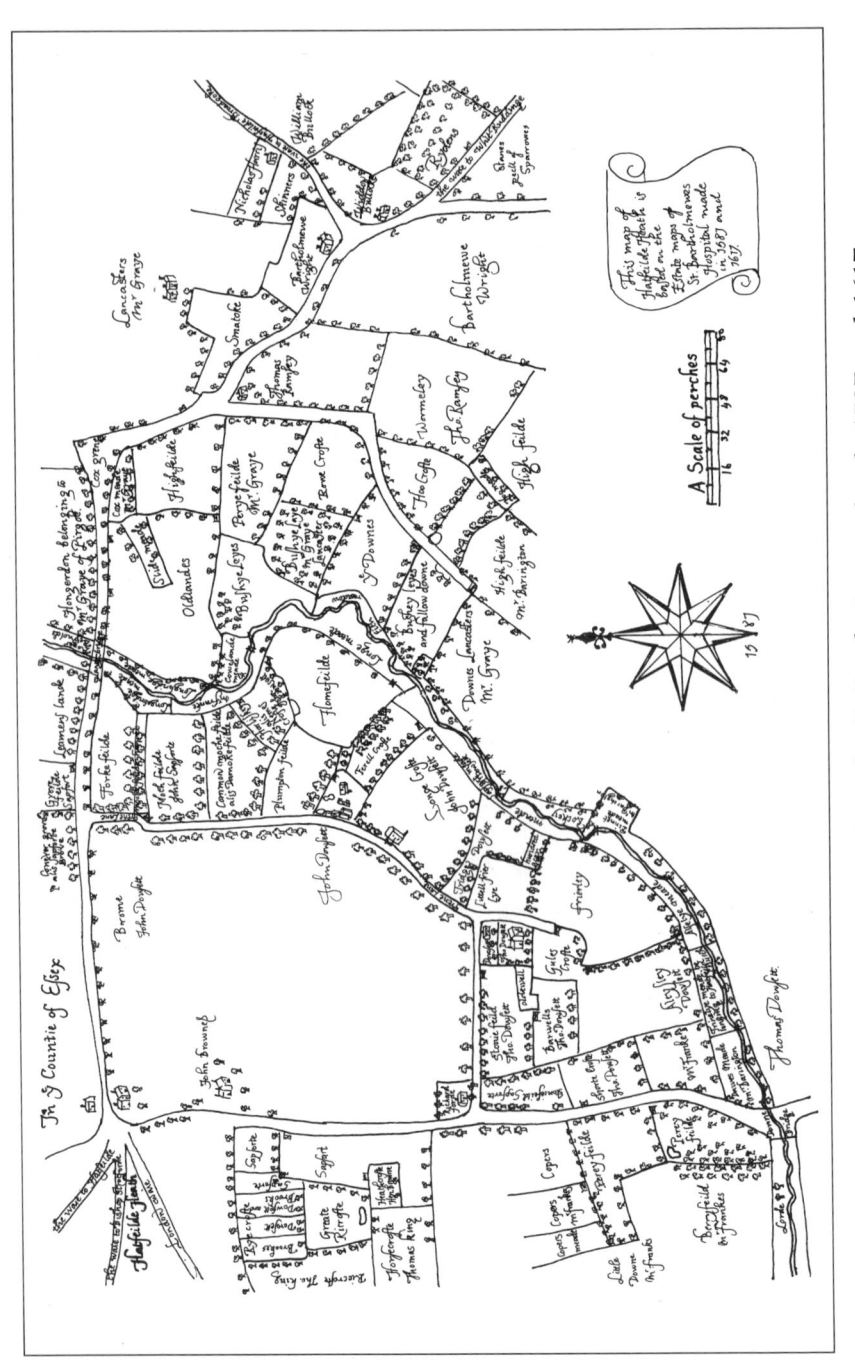

Composite Map based on the St Bartholomew lands 1587 and 1617

Windmill on Hatfield Heath with auxiliary engine shed.

Hawkins coal depot next to the Stag taken at the end of the 19th. century.

Button's harness makers shop (now Beehive cottage).

Manse cottages at the turn of the century. Note the common practice of keeping livestock on the Heath.

View of the Heath showing the Duplex oil lamps.

Griggs Lane (Mill Lane) with Alfred Little's stables on the right of picture.

Moat cottage on the south side of the Heath. Possible site of Dame school. Mrs F Bruty and Mrs W Bruty in the doorways and Sophie Bruty standing by the gate.

Charlie Mills's boot repair shop next to Davis Row.

(II)
The Churches

"Tarry no longer! Towards thine heritage.
Haste on they way, and be of good cheer
Go each day onward on they pilgrimage
Thy place is bigger above the starres clear,
Think how short time thou shall abide here,
None earthly palace wrought in so stately wise
Come on, my friend, my brother most entire.
For Thee I offered my blood in sacrifice."

John Lydgate. Prior. Hatfield Broad Oak 1423.

CONGREGATIONAL/UNITED REFORMED CHURCH

On St Bartholomew's Day 24th August 1662 some two thousand clergy left their livings as they felt unable to assent to the Act of Uniformity and between 400 to 500 then became know as 'Independents'. One of these, the Rev. John Warren, was expelled from Hatfield Broad Oak Church and came to the Heath to build up a non-conformist fellowship. He remained for 28 years before moving to Bishop's Stortford and founding the Independent Church there. John Warren was described by his contemporaries as a remarkable man, one of sound judgement, a very kind and considerate christian and an able preacher, not at all the ecclesiastical revolutionary one might have thought. He once had the honour of preaching to Parliament, and served on the Commission of Ejection, which looked into clergy competence, both appointments probably coming through his connection with the Barrington family.

The Church appears to have met first in the house of Anne Parker situated on the west side of the Heath. A move was made to a converted barn under the Ministry of Rev. James Small, chaplain to Sir John Barrington, this barn being leased from Thomas Stacey. Then, in 1726 during the ministry of Rev. George Wiggett, and with the congregation greatly increased to over 300 worshippers, a new chapel was built on the present site on land purchased by Mr Wiggett from William Green of Gt. Waltham. This was enhanced by the building of the Manse (now Gowrie House) in 1730. There then followed a very successful ministry under the Rev. Thomas Cawdwell who remained for 34 years, and it was during this time that the Church changed its affiliation from Presbyterian

A History of Hatfield Heath

to Congregational. In this period the Church had the support of several prominent families in the district including the Joscelynes (Sir Strange and Sir Conyers) of Hyde Hall, the Welhams of Moor Hall and Madam Mico of Campions together with the original trustees, H Longbottom of Hallingbury Park, M Green, J Parker, S Lord, G Dorrington, J Brookes, J Perry, B Sapsford, J Scruby and others.

During Rev. Cawdwell's ministry a remarkable man, Thomas Porter, became a member of his congregation. Although unable to read or write and with an impaired intellect he was able to quote long passages from the Bible through hearing the word from his minister and the congregation. In addition he was gifted in being able to select and collate the text most appropriate for the occasion. His fame spread near and far and he was often summoned by the gentry to give a demonstration of these gifts.

The Rev. Isaac Henley was the Minister from 1765 to 1777 and his chief contribution was the running of a successful school at his house. In order to accommodate the increasing number of pupils, the Church added more rooms to what became known as the 'Parsonage House'. It looks as if Mr Henley was a better schoolteacher than minister as the congregation declined in this period. Then, under the Rev. Samuel Gaffee who came straight from Homerton College and stayed for 28 years, the membership greatly increased. The Rev. Gaffee according to his contemporaries was "a man of eminent piety and most affectionate disposition," and was very popular with his entire congregation. Galleries were added to the building both in 1788 and in 1804 through the generosity of Mr Little of Sheering Mill and with the help of members.

The Rev. Cornelius Berry followed Samuel Gaffee and holds the record for the longest serving ministry in the Church's history, 53 years, from 1811 - 1864. The Rev. Berry was a man devoted to his charge at the Heath and was universally beloved and respected. This seems to have been a time of great expansion in many directions. The Evangelical Revival had affected the churches and caused an increase in the number of Independent Churches in the country. Mr Berry played his part even encouraging his own members to join churches in Takeley and Sawbridgeworth and founded Chapels both in Hatfield Broad Oak and Matching Tye around the year 1818. Although this involved losses to the church on the Heath these new churches grew stronger as did their mother Church, for in 1830 the Chapel was again enlarged at a cost of £202. In 1829 authorisation for a burial ground behind the chapel was obtained.

The Churches

Another development around this time was the Church's concern for education. A school based on the 'British' system was started in 1834 attended only on a Sunday. Around 1857 a day school, called The British School was built at a cost of £400 and open to pupils of all denominations, the greater part of the cost being raised by the congregation. This building was enlarged to accommodate another classroom in 1897. Around 1860 an evening class was started for the adults of the village, both schoolings being controlled by a Board of Managers appointed by the Church. A new Trust Deed was made on 1st December 1868 for the governance of Church and School. H Girling of Harlow and SP Matthews of Campions were the retiring trustees reappointed, and W Poole of Sawbridgeworth, SS Poole of Matching Hall, TH Poole of Pierce Williams, John and Thomas Brown, of Lt. Hallingbury Hall, C Martin of Matching Tye, John Hockley of Friars, TW Brown of Crabbs Green, Cornelius Nash of Broad Oak, the Petts family from Stock Hall and W Hutchin and W Witham from the Heath later formed the new board members. Miss Susannah Poole of Matching Hall and then Oaklands was also a staunch supporter of both the Heath and Matching churches at this time, as were FR Matthews and JP Matthews of Housham Tye. It was through the generosity of Joseph P Matthews that the new Matching Tye chapel was built in 1875, one year after his death.

The work of the Church continued to grow under the Rev. GE Singleton and in 1869 the burial ground at the rear of the chapel was extended through land purchased from Barnard Matthews of Gibsons. It was during this time that the present building was erected, with the foundation stone being laid on 29th June 1875 together with a bottle containing artefacts of the time. The chapel opened thirteen months later at a cost of £3,304 plus £500 for the organ. The architect was T Lewis Banks and the builder W Cornwell. One of the special features of the new building is the beautiful stained glass window depicting the life of St. Paul which was dedicated to the memory of the Rev. Cornelius Berry, whose ministry paved the way towards the construction of the new chapel, although he did not live to see it completed. The first wedding held in the new chapel was between Mr William Stalley of the USA and Mary Hutchin on 22nd February 1879. In 1883 the church acquired three cottages on the Heath which were gifts from JR Matthews and Miss F Brown of Campions. This bequest was an alternative proposal to that of the late Mr SP Matthews of Housham Hall Matching who had left a small farm at White Roding but this had met with certain legal difficulties. In the same year the deacons were able to purchase the two brick cottages and the thatched cottage situated between the chapel and the Manse for a sum of £370.

A History of Hatfield Heath

Over the past one hundred and twenty-five years, since building the new chapel, there have been twelve appointed ministers including the Rev. Robert Jude who served here for the first 24 years of the century. His wife died in 1973 at the age of 100. Their daughter Gwen was also very involved in the life of the village. Around this time a church member, the Rev. Herbert George Brown became a distinguished Congregational minister. He married Alice Hockley daughter of John Hockley Snr on 1st October 1898 and served the church for a long period at Tewkesbury where he became Mayor of the Borough. In 1930 Richard Martin Broad and Edward Rogers were made life Elders and in 1934 Mrs. Hockley and Mrs. Buck became the church's first women deacons.

In between the wars the church was to experience several changes in regard to its future. It accepted a gift in 1922 from Mr WS Poole, of two cottages, which were made into one and used by Mr Rogers as the school masters house. His daughter, Doris lived in this house all her life and was known for her fine soprano voice. A magazine for the church was started in 1925, edited by Mr Hunt. The satellite chapel at Hatfield Broad Oak built in 1868 and which had been used as soldiers' reading room in the 1st World War was let as a men's club from 1929. In 1939 this building became the Roman Catholic Church. The British School was merged in 1932 with the Church of England National School and came under the authority of the Essex County Council. The old school building then became known as the Congregational Hall, although part of it was converted for residential use. Under the ministry of the Rev. White, electricity was installed in the church in 1936, a gift from Mary Agnes Broad in memory of her late husband and son. The Rev. White's first wife Dorothy was a very active church member as was his second wife Gwen who attended the church well into her 90th year.

The church celebrated its Tercentenary in 1962 with special services and in the same year also sold the old Manse (Gowrie House). Four years later the very popular Minister the Rev. Sidney Wheale moved into the new Manse at Hurst Lea. This was eventually sold in 1984 together with Manse Cottages and then the old school house next to the church became the new home of the incumbents. The church was able to celebrate the centenary of the present building in June 1975 with a service broadcast on the BBC Radio 4 "Service of Worship", which was conducted by the Minister, the Rev. Frank Mead.

The chapel was re-roofed in 1981 by which time the bell tower was found to be in a dangerous state, therefore in 1982 it was taken down and a new cross was mounted on the modified steeple. It was designed by a member, Mrs Anne Broad and cast at Raine foundry. In 1984 the old school building was

The Churches

demolished and a new church hall, kitchen and toilets built. The Hall was opened by the former church secretary Richard Nanscawen Broad on 16th February 1985. Mr Broad had served as secretary from 1929 to 1974 and was succeeded by his son Martin Broad, secretary for twelve years. Geoffrey Broad also had a very long connection with the Church going back to 1951, first as auditor then treasurer followed by pulpit secretary. The organ received an overhaul in 1992 from a legacy left by Harry King who was a resident of the village in his younger days. In 1997 a Garden of Remembrance was created within the graveyard and planted with ornamental trees, a gift from the Leisure Hour.

It would be impossible to record all that the Church owes to the large number of people throughout the years who have worked and maintained the Witness in this village's life. There are, however, many people who have given outstanding service over the years to the local Non Conformist cause. In the 19th Century the Girling, the Browns, the Pooles, the Hockleys, the Nashs, the Eades and the Matthews families were all stalwarts of a growing Church. Frederick Barker, the local undertaker and then his son Ernest Barker looked after church maintenance. Alice Barker undertook cleaning for many years and was followed by Jessie Adams and then Mrs Gunn. Mr Hutchin and Mrs Bruty succeeded them in 1920. In the first half of the 20th Century the Hockley family, the Broads, the Bowyers, the Lukies of Cammas Hall, Mr and Mrs Bogie, the Scantleburys of Parvilles, the Hutchins and the Sapsfords together with the Bucks, Lakeys, Reynolds, Rogers, Vales and Thomas and Graham Glasse of Little Laver were to continue the Witness of non-conformism here. A women's meeting has been held within the church for many years and after a lapse during the 1st World War was re-formed by Mrs E Rogers, Mrs A Hockley, Mrs E Vale and the Minister's wife Mrs Davies, together with the help of Mesdames Scantlebury, Buck, Dix, Liddell, Gunn, Day, Bruty, D Broad and G Hutchin. Later Mesdames D White, Bogie, Glasse, Herald, Lakey, Sayers, M Clarke and W Want would all take a part in this fellowship.

During the 1960's the work in the church was taken up by Mr and Mrs Reg Clarke, Winnie Want, Gilbert Hutchin, Mrs Sayer, Mr Webb, Richard and Violet Griffiths, Mr and Mrs Jack Waller, Jim and Rene Liddell of Shrubbs, John Lukies, George and Nellie Brown and Mr and Mrs Canfield of Lt. Hallingbury. In more recent times Frank Prior has completed 30 years as fabric steward and Roland Strutt (30 years an Elder), Ken Bennison, the Dean family, Ted Collins and Catharine Cook all participate as lay preachers while Lily Barker continues the long succession of her family in the service of the Church as 'Together' magazine distributor. This is produced by Dinah Hutchin with help from Pat

A History of Hatfield Heath

Hustings and Margaret Perry. Judy Lemon has held the office of flower secretary for over 20 years when taking over the work from Nellie Brown who herself served for many years in this position. Gwen Ellis, a former Elder, has had for many years the responsibility of distributing church flowers to the sick and needy, work also carried out with dedication by Doreen Millen. Currently Olwyn Evans holds the Women's Meeting chair and Miriam Fenn the treasurership. In 1965 Mrs Grace Wheale the minister's wife started an evening leisure group which is still going strong today chaired for more than 25 years by Jean Wybrew with Dinah Hutchin as secretary and Margaret Perry the treasurer. A Young Peoples' fellowship was run between the wars and a youth club was formed in the 1950s, a forerunner of the present Children's Club held on Fridays.

In 1972 members voted to join the new United Reformed Church, and its links with Matching Tye were therefore finally ended. In 1980 Hatfield Heath was grouped with the URC Churches at High and Good Easter. As with most churches there has been a dramatic decline in attendance since the First World War. At present there are 60 members and it is administered through the Chelmsford District of the Eastern Provence of the United Reformed Church. The Rev. Margaret Taylor was appointed as minister in 1987 and was the first woman to hold the position until her retirement in 1997. For the next two years the secretary, Roland Strutt, the elders and members, undertook the work of the Church in the district. In September 1999 the Rev Nigel Rogers was appointed minister on a shared basis with the Little Waltham and High Easter churches

LIST OF SERVING MINISTERS

Rev. John Warren MA	1662 - 1694	Rev. RC Jude	1899 - 1923
Rev. James Small	1694 - 1707	Rev. WE Davies	1924 - 1931
Rev. George Wiggett	1707 - 1728	Rev. EE Marks	1931 - 1934
Rev. Thomas Cawdwell	1731 -1765	Rev. R White	1935 - 1944
Rev. Isaac Henley	1765 - 1777	Rev. PJ Lawton BA	1945 - 1954
Rev. Samuel Gaffee	1780 - 1808	Rev. FC Milne	1955 - 1961
Rev. Cornelius Berry	1811 - 1864	Rev W S Wheale	1963 - 1971
Rev. GE Singleton	1864 - 1883	Rev. FA Mead	1972 - 1979
Rev. JS Morley	1884 - 1893	Rev. J Hannah	1981 - 1985
Rev. ER Palmer	1893 - 1898	Rev. M Taylor	1987 - 1997
		Rev. N Rogers	1999 -

The Churches

Holy Trinity

The Parish Church of Holy Trinity was built in 1859 on land given by Alan Lowndes MA, DL the Lord of the Manor, and with considerable effort undertaken earlier by the Rev. T Hall and by the parishioners of the Mother Church of St. Mary's Hatfield Broad Oak. At the same time they built a church at Bush End where Miss Sarah Chamberlayne of Ryes provided much of the finance. Originally the parish was under the Diocese of Rochester with the Bishop of Rochester consecrating the churchyard on 4th August 1859. In 1877 it was transferred to St Albans, and finally in 1914 to the new Diocese of Chelmsford.

The church consists of a chancel and nave with a broached tower and spire on the south side; this contained three bells cast in 1857. There were originally two stained glass windows, one presented by Mr D Williams of The Grange and the other in memory of Mary daughter of the Rev. T Hall. The Rev. Hall lost his young son and his daughter both within the same month in 1844. The church was improved in 1883 when a south aisle was added and it then seated 210. The wooden pulpit was replaced in 1903 by one of stone in memory of Lord Rookwood (Selwin Ibbertson) of Down Hall who died in 1902, and who was for many years a churchwarden along with John Pamphilon and Arthur Millbank. To commemorate the Church's Jubilee in 1909 a two-manual organ was installed at a cost of £300 and a grand fete was held in the vicarage grounds. The beautiful east window was given by Mrs Horace Broke of Gladwyns and later the wrought iron lectern was given by friends in memory of her late husband. A stained glass window in memory of the Horsey family was dedicated by the Bishop of Barking in 1954.

Twenty years after the building of the church, in 1879, the Parish Visitation recorded "three bells in the church but two cracked". It seemed that they had fairly recently been hung in wheels to allow them to be rung in peal. Three years later only one was cracked so presumably the church had managed to repair one of the bells. By 1881 the hanging was defective and in 1893 they were no longer hung for peal ringing. From 1898 there were two "quite new" bells, but from the turn of the century the bells were chimed only. The six bells currently installed at Holy Trinity were recast at the Whitechapel Bell Foundry in 1961 from the metal from the original three bells which had been made there in 1897/8. The recasting resulted in a peal of six lightweight bells, the Treble weighing just over 2 cwt. while the Tenor weighed a little over 4 cwt. The first peal was rung on 1st July 1961 the ringers being: Reginald Hayden; Treble, Henry Bird, 2, Edward Curzon, 3, John Collins, 4, Edward Rochester, 5, William Aley, Tenor. The present Captain of the Tower is Gerald

A History of Hatfield Heath

Pearson and it is interesting to note that two of the youngest ringers in 1999, Daniel and Michael Collins are great-nephews of John Collins who rang the inaugural peal on the six bells in 1961.

In 1863 the building, now called the Institute, was erected on its present site for use as the Church School and Hall with accommodation for 140 children. An earlier National School had been in operation on the Heath since 1840. However with a greatly increased demand within the parish and after much hard work, in which the sum of £1,500 was raised, a new church school building was opened in 1900 on the site opposite the Church under the mastership of CW Sharp. The corrugated steel building, originally known as the Parish Hall and later the Trinity Hall, was given to the church by Lord and Lady Rookwood. It was opened on 27th November 1894 by Lord Lambourne (Col. Mark Lockwood MP). The smaller room known as the Annexe was believed to have been originally utilised as a school before being moved to the other side of the Heath opposite Davis Row. Here it was occupied by a Betty Robinson and its corrugated sides caused much entertainment for any child with a stick, to the amusement of the neighbours upon Betty's spirited reaction! This building was later condemned and moved to Sheering where it was 'rescued' by Mrs Horace Broke and attached to Trinity Hall as an annexe.

In 1926 the management of Trinity Hall, which after 1921 had been the responsibility of the PCC, was transferred to a Committee of Representatives from several village organisations with EE Hockley as hon. secretary and later JJ Button and then AEG Search. At that time the Hall was still church property. From 1900 the Institute was run as a Men's Club and reading room by a village committee comprising Lord Rookwood, Horace Broke, the Vicar and twelve elected members, this arrangement being confirmed by the Dioceses of St. Albans and Chelmsford in 1923. The Institute building was extended in 1929 due to the generosity of BTR Pyle of Town Grove and this enabled the village library to expand under Ralph Dix. A Mothers' Meeting was held on Tuesday afternoons in the Institute for many years and before the 1st World War a clothing club and a coal club were organised. In the 1920's a Mothers' Union and a Women's Fellowship were formed.

During the 2nd World War the church saw a good deal of 'active service'. A bomb destroyed the 'Church Gate' house to the north of the church and damaged the Institute wall. Trinity Hall was used temporarily as a school for the evacuees from London. After the war electricity was installed in the church and the bomb damaged Institute wall repaired. The south transept was dedicated as a war memorial chapel. In the fifties the boundaries to the

The Churches

churchyard were extended and enclosed after years of legal negotiation. At this time too, Trinity Hall was extended at the rear and underwent refurbishment.

The church celebrated the centenary of its building in August 1959 with a series of concerts, socials, fetes and services culminating with Evensong on 9th August followed by a morality play by TB Morris performed by parishioners. In 1968 Trinity Hall was leased for the benefit of the Village Hall Trust, and was replaced by the present Village Hall in 1970. In 1975 the Institute was also leased to the Trust for a term of 49 years. A new vicarage was built in the grounds of the old victorian vicarage in 1979. Later this old house became the offices of the Sarbir company.

Over the years Holy Trinity has had many devoted servants. Daniel Day was Parish Clerk from 1884 to 1932, and during most of that time maintained the churchyard and Institute hall in excellent condition, he died in 1936 and was succeeded by Percy Newman. Another parishioner giving long and devoted service was Clara Coleman who served as PCC secretary from 1921 to 1975. On her retirement she was presented with a Minton china tea service and a scroll in recognition of her services to the parish. Miss Coleman also had the honour, in 1963, of receiving Maundy Money from the Queen at Chelmsford Cathedral as recognition of her services to the Church. The Broke family had very long associations with Holy Trinity; Lt. Col. H Broke was People's Warden from 1909 when he took over from Mr Bretton, and Edward Perry, son of the village blacksmith Walter Perry of Forge Cottage, was Vicar's Warden from 1905 to 1931. Montrose Stuart, schoolmaster, was organist for many years and was succeeded by Miss EK Harris. The Gladwyns' connection continued when PV Broke succeeded his brother in 1923 and served for some 23 years along side Squadron Leader Wordsworth. After the war the churchwardens were Mr Dix, Headmaster, and Mr Bloxome of Peggerells.

On the 1st January 1990 the parish was united with that of St. Mary the Virgin, Sheering to form the United Benefice of Hatfield Heath and Sheering. In 1999, to celebrate the Millennium, a group of church members came together to make a set of runners for the choir stall seats in tapestry. All the symbols used reflect different aspects of the spiritual life of the church.

Holy Trinity, within the United Benefice, has continued to worship God and witness His love and to this end has, over 140 years, been served by many faithful followers within the parish.

A History of Hatfield Heath

VICARS OF HOLY TRINITY

A Crofts-Bullen	1859 - 1862	WH Holdsworth	1927 - 1933
TG Postlewaite	1862 - 1877	E Allen	1933 - 1936
AE Beaven	1877 - 1885	AF Gardiner	1936 - 1945
JL Green	1885 - 1893	FB Horsey	1945 - 1955
TW Ward	1893 - 1897	FH Roberts	1956 - 1962
TW Reynolds	1897 - 1905	R Smythe	1962 - 1978
H De V Watson	1905 - 1915	W Dickinson	1978 - 1986
EA Du Cane	1915 - 1927	T Potter	1987 -

This chapter illustrates the important part played by both churches over the years in enriching the lives of the people of Hatfield Heath. The development of 'Church' and 'Chapel' and their schools was unique in a village of this size. Although there has often been differences of opinion and of approach a spirit of friendship and co-operation has grown steadily over the years.

Old Chapel (on right) built in 1726 beside the school house (built in 1857) on the Chelmsford Road.

Chelmsford Road and the URC church showing the old Bell Tower.

Harvest Festival at the Congregational Chapel in the early years of the Century

Recasting the bells for Holy Trinity Church 1961.

Oak tree outside Holy Trinity church which provided a focal point for the church and village activities, damaged by fire lit by "a boy called Brown" in 1899.

Welcome Club Christmas Dinner 1957

Scout Summer Camp at Brent Pelham 1949. Bob Bucknell, Mike Saban, John White, David Wilkinson and 'Skipper' Clark.

National School in 1899 taken outside the Institute just before the school transferred to the new building. All the boys with headmaster Mr Montrose Stuart.

National School pupils outside the new school with headmaster Mr CW Sharp.

National School children digging for victory during the 1st. World War on a plot beside the school.

Pupils and staff of the British School taken at the end of the 19th. century. Possibly Rev. Palmer and Mr Carson, headmaster.

Staff of the Central Kitchen which provided meals for 12 local schools. Violet Bedell, Jessie Adams, Fred Bruty, Jean Bruty, Dorothy Search.

Mark Ilott (Essex CCC) with Sophie Best and Tom Plane opening the new school building on 4th. April 1995 (Herts & Essex Observer).

School children collecting their Coronation spoons from Peacock's shop May 1937.

(111)
The Schools

Miss Jane Aitkin - Certificated Teacher
Miss Hannah Branch - Pupil Teacher

The rate of failure is not high for a Country School like this, 11.4%. More than one third of the Children presented were in the three higher standards and this is a very creditable proportion. The instruction of the Pupil Teacher does the Mistress credit.

Matthew Arnold, School Inspector,
Poet and eldest son of Dr. Arnold, Headmaster of Rugby.
Hatfield Heath British School Inspection; April 1867.

It was at about the beginning of the nineteenth century that schooling began to be available to all children of Hatfield Broad Oak and Hatfield Heath. Before this there had been a number of Dame Schools, Charity Schools, Sunday Schools and others including, in 1564, a "School for Gentry," and in 1769 a shoemaker's wife had opened a school in Hatfield Heath. It was with the opening of the British school (Nonconformist) here in 1857, attached to the Congregational Church, and the National School, under the Church of England in 1863 that the long advance to universal education began. Some of the logbooks kept by those two foundations are still available. From these may be extracted the story of the gradual advance of education locally since those times.

Ever since the Middle Ages bishops had had authority over schools. It appears to have been unlawful to teach without their permission. A case in point is that in 1686, a tailor, John Threder, "was accused of teaching certain children in the house of John Threder without license from the Bishop." Two labourers were indicted for aiding and abetting him. The Anglicans founded the National Society for " promoting the education of the poor in the principles of the Established Church." Teaching was largely based on the Bible.

Government support began in 1833 with a small grant for these two societies, British Schools and National Schools. School Boards were formed in 1870 and these stipulated that religious education should be non-sectarian and based on the Bible, an important proviso in those troublesome sectarian times. This led to minor difficulties; thus "James Dior was expelled from the Baptist membership for having his children baptised at the Parish Church so that they could go to the Church School." Inevitably there was rivalry. In 1839 the vicar considered the nonconformist school to be a "hindrance to the development of the Church school."

In 1848 the nonconformist master, aged 18, received a salary of six shillings per week (£15 per annum) plus twopence for each child. By his third year his annual salary had reached £30. In 1890 Mr Alfred Collar was paid £33 plus half of the school pence and in 1892 Mr Carson, who held a teaching certificate from Borough Road Training College in London received £80. In 1862 the system of payment by results had been introduced based on the scholars' attainments; thus the teachers' salary became dependent on the performance of the children at the school's annual inspection as measured by Her Majesty's Inspector of Schools on one particular day of the year. A copy of the report appears for each year in the school logbook and they vary from severe through threatening (to reduce the grant) to fairly mild.

Children were expected to pay school fees and these were levied on a sliding scale starting at a few pence for the first child and reducing according to how many children in the family attended school down to no payment for the youngest. In 1858 at the British School 34 boys paid 1d. per week 62 girls paid 1d. and 17 girls paid 2d. The rate of payment depending on the means of the parents. One mistress received £13 p.a. while another, who was certificated, was engaged for £40 p.a.

In the 1870s the prosperity of arable farming declined and many farms were in a deplorable condition, many verging on bankruptcy. This reflected on village life and attempts to relieve poverty were noted as in the record book in 1901; "Six children are away, gone to Down Hall for soup." Thus we see heavy absenteeism from school with frequent entries deploring the poor attendance. Parents and employers often regarded school attendance as a barrier to the family income with children going to school and not being available for such activities as bird scaring. School holidays were aligned to the farming year and its demands with harvest and gleaning much to the fore. In times of hardship a woman could glean enough grain in the autumn to keep her in bread for the winter.

Illness took a heavy toll especially in the winter. The school was often closed for some weeks during not infrequent outbreaks of scarlet fever, mumps, measles, German measles, diphtheria, scarletina and whooping cough;

ailments which could be fatal. Thus; "School closed from Jan. 6th to March 3rd. then reclosed until March 17th because of measles." In 1893 "Closed from Dec. 18th to Jan. 15th, scarlet fever." Besides these diseases appear an assortment of other reasons for absence: "consumption, broke his arm, bitten by a dog, excluded (head lice?), kicked by a horse, operation for his throat, (tonsillitis or diphtheria) neuralgia, ringworm, scabies, infectious sores, "the itch," and blood poisoning." Sadly a death is recorded; "Amos Eaton died at noon." Also; "bad weather, harvesting, gleaning, looking after the baby, chopped off the end of his thumb, no shoes." Appearance at school barefoot was not unusual, however, and there is mention of a "boot club" to ease the financial burden for parents and from 1811 there had been a "clothing club." In 1897 one child attended school so infrequently that it was recorded when he did attend! "Cleo Eaton came to school."

By 1895 a School Attendance Officer had been appointed and he is recorded as serving a summons on one mother for the poor attendance of her son. Another indication of the amount of poverty at the time can possibly be found in the entry; "11 were absent on a begging expedition.... this disgraceful thing occurs every few months.... allowed and encouraged by their parents."

Mentions of absences are frequent, but one admittance was made to ensure the attendance of the rest of the family; "Ernest W Day admitted, only will not be 3 years old until Nov. 30th. Mother says she will have to keep her other two at home to look after her younger child if EW Day cannot come."

In 1916 there is the first mention of "Medical Inspection" the day of the school doctor had arrived. Visits by the school dentist commenced around 1920 or earlier. In April 1867 the British school was inspected by Matthew Arnold, the poet whose father was headmaster of Rugby school and appeared in "Tom Brown's Schooldays." He visited the school five times between 1867 and 1871 signing the logbook each time except in 1869. His reports are copied into the logbook and are distinguished by the language being more encouraging and gentler than other Inspectors of his day.

The Vicar or Minister usually chaired the Management Body, but the Head Teacher was in daily charge with the assistance of some other staff. It seemed usual to appoint a Headmaster, with his wife as his assistant to teach the Infants and to take the sewing classes with the girls, while the boys took drawing or some other form of art. The local gentry were much to the fore on the managing bodies. In 1891 the National School Managers consisted of; Rt. Hon. Sir Henry Selwin Ibbetson Bart. MP (treasurer), Lady Eden Selwin Ibbetson,

A History of Hatfield Heath

Rev. Laurence Green MA Vicar, (correspondent), while the staff comprised; Edwin Alfred Cates, Certificated First Class, Mary Ann Cates, Article 68 and Edith Mary E Cates, Monitor. The Vicar and Managers visited the school frequently and occasionally took a lesson, writing a note in the log book and checking the registers; "Attendance not quite as good as usual. Vicar took Geography" In 1901 "Lord and Lady Rookwood visited the school".

The relationship between the Head and managers was not always amicable. On 5th April 1890 Mr JH Dixon was given three months notice in writing by the managers. The British School Council minutes and the Head's log book give different accounts of this rift, the council minutes recording that complaints had been made about his excessive strictness while Mr Dixon claims that no adequate reason was given for what was in his eyes unfair dismissal. In spite of this the HMI report for that year, written on May 13th, was a very good one; "Passes are up from 70% to 84.9%.... greatest improvement in Arithmetic during his tenure from 70% to 81%.... unremitting attention to school work.... marked improvement in discipline.... neatness of work.... up 15%." He left on 20th. June with the plaudits of the managers at the school's end-of-year gathering ringing in his ears!

At the beginning of each term a list of songs to be taught was given together with a list of "object lessons." An object lesson was one where the focal point was, for example, a piece of coal, a nest, a leather strap and so on. The children were expected to sit upright, hands behind them, and reply to a series of questions from the teacher, starting from; "What is that? Where did it come from? Hands up..." all the children remaining mute in case they drew down the wrath of the teacher for a wrong answer. Six songs were listed, for example "Hearts of Oak", "Here's a Health unto his Majesty", and "Cheerfulness". Object lessons included; A Straw Hat, A Potato, Clothing, in all about twenty four objects. Repetition included an extract from "The Merchant of Venice" and "The Boy who told a Lie", no doubt a poem with a heavy moral theme.

Timetables were important, having to be submitted, approved and followed, or a reason given in the logbook. Typically they would include; Singing, Prayers, and Scripture, Arithmetic, Writing, Spelling, Playtime, Reading, Drawing, Needlework, Geography, Tables, Grammar. In 1892 lecturers on Ambulance (first aid?) for boys and cooking for girls were included and evening classes are mentioned in 1898. By 1900 Elementary Science makes an appearance, in 1903 Physical Training and in 1906 Gardening are added. By 1912 the girls were attending cookery classes in Dunmow.

The Schools

From the above bare bones HMI commented at length on many aspects; In 1891 these included discipline, efficiency, reading "some faults in style" Handwriting "want of neatness and accuracy" Dictation, Composition, "very serious defects" Mental Arithmetic, Meanings and "illusions of poetry," General Intelligence..... Infants had separate mention; Reading, "ought not to be repeated a word at a time, but to phrase more."

The Religious Education inspection was carried out by a separately appointed cleric. These reports were, on the whole, good, glowing with words like "excellent, extremely well" to "whole class answering with spirit" for the Infants. Some other HMI Reports were condemnatory though, concluding with wording such as, "His Majesty's Inspectors will look for much improvement (in this or that area) when the school is inspected next year," together with dire warnings that there would be "reductions in the Government Grant should there not be an improvement the following year." Unfortunately the following year they wrote; "Because of defective arithmetic My Lords have made a deduction from the grant under Article 52, we will hope to find evidence of improved instruction next year."

In 1863 the British School HMI Reports were based on, amongst other things; Cleanliness of premises, Reading, Mental Arithmetic, Geography, (the main features of Great Britain) Dictation, Sewing, Singing, and Grammar. By 1867, things had improved with remarks such as "very creditable" and "higher standards". Arithmetic seems to have been the perennial stumbling block. In 1880 the HMI report stated; "the grant is to be reduced by one tenth because of the unfavourable report in the Arithmetic of the school.... they will look for general improvement in the course next year." One head complained upon the general crassness of the HMI questions to the pupils such as "What do the people in Russia do?" and to the Infants "Is a cat bigger or less than a horse, a cow, or a mouse?" However another point of view is shown by the entry of Mr Thomas Price in 1895 complaining, as a new head, "Children hardly knew any arithmetic when I arrived here I have now spent a week teaching St. III (Standard III) long division and the bulk of the class seem as far off from understanding the rule as they were in the beginning.... not being conversant with their tables.... In subtraction they forget to borrow and pay back."

Teaching staff elsewhere were commented on by HMI favourably or unfavourably. Teacher's certificates could be up or downgraded every five years. On one a "Miss --- is to be congratulated on" whereas another teacher is urged to be "more rigorous". Again we have "more brightness on the part of the teacher" One pupil teacher was criticised by Matthew Arnold; "The pupil teacher's grammar is so bad that it will be impossible to pass her again unless it improves." In her third year she was again criticised for Geography and History and the issuing of her certificate was deferred. Heads themselves were, not infrequently, critical of their predecessors upon taking up their office. One, writing in the logbook, said that he found pupils "backward in everything ...... discipline flaccid" and ended with a statement of his determination to improve maths during his time of tenure. Both schools were subject to this procedure. Arithmetic seemed to receive the most critical mention. In 1884 the Inspectors noted that "The Infant teacher is not equal to anything beyond the rudiments of reading, writing, arithmetic and needlework." In 1893 it was "Timetable not adhered to ...... discipline moderate ...... average ability, reading very fast and monotonous ...... writing no uniformity of style."

School premises and needs were commented on; thus in 1876 new slates, bibles and blotting paper were requested and blackboards were to be painted. By 1883 larger framed slates were advised. 1892 we see "Desks too high ...... gallery seats want backs ...... a cleaner path to the door ...... a larger scraper ...... clothes ought not to be left on the floor." In the following year; "Closets might advantageously be emptied every quarter" and "Each of the closets should have a door" In 1893 reference was made to "the prison like appearance owing to clear glass not being used" and in 1898 the complaint was that "the offices (lavatories) smell abominably and are very near the school." In 1897 the British School was enlarged at a cost of £59 financed by a loan from Gibson and Tukes Bank but the Inspectors in 1909 still had cause to comment "Window cills 6ft to 9ft high and do not open ...... Playground is too small, additional site needed."

During the earlier years there is mention in the logs of both schools of "Boarding Out children." These children, it seems, were from London Boroughs taken into care and sent here to be fostered out and to attend local schools. One of these, Harry King, had no name when he came being but an infant. He was boarded with a family who lived in the farmhouse down Mill Lane and was given the surname after a local family. He worked there as a farm worker and gardener until the First World War when he joined the army and was wounded on the Somme. He must have had happy memories of his time here at the British School as upon retirement he visited the village and left, in gratitude, a legacy to the Congregational Church together with a grant towards the maintenance of the War Memorial.

In 1895 Mr and Mrs Rogers were appointed to the British School at a remuneration of £80 p.a. and a free house. They effected a great improvement and stayed for twenty-six years. When they arrived there were 65 on roll but an

The Schools

average attendance of only 38. Results were bad indeed as shown from a test Mr Rogers conducted. By 1898 HMI gave a very good report saying "a very good and successful teacher." Even the stumbling block of arithmetic was described as "excellent." Of Mrs Rogers they said, "Infants carefully taught." Mr Rogers retired in 1921.

> This stone was laid by
> Henry Montague Butler DD
> Master of Trinity College Cambridge
> Wednesday 25 October 1899
> EH Hockley Builder.

The above is a copy of the wording on the foundation stone of the present school. William Fowler MP opened this school on 1st August 1900 and the National School, previously housed in the Village Institute, then moved across the road to its new building. The new school, handsome and well built, had a schoolhouse attached. It was described as a "3 class school with cloakrooms attached." There would have been open fires for heating and oil lamps for lighting. A bell hung above two substantial outer doors whose stone lintels were engraved with "Boys" on one and "Girls and Infants" on the other leading into separate cloakrooms. Later, solid fuel "tortoise" stoves were installed with radiators in every room. Electric lighting replaced gas lighting in 1949 and later still, in the 70's natural gas replaced solid fuel with the heating system now being fully automated. No longer do we see log book entries like one in September 1914, "Mrs Day sent her boy, Fred Herald, to light the fires .... with his usual aptitude for bungling his work he managed to choke up the stove .... we were almost smothered with smoke." Appearing in the log from 1900, "Total expenditure on the New School was £181-0-2 $^1/_2$, not £181-1-2 $^1/_2$ as stated."

Numbers on roll started around 50 but fell to 25 by 1932. At this stage questions were raised as to the viability of such a small number warranting a school and ought it to be closed? The solution was obvious. The British School closed and the scholars transferred to the newer school on 4th April 1932. Mr Ralph Dix, headmaster of the Nondenominational school, became headmaster bringing with him 62 pupils to join 25 of the C of E school plus 2 new children, making a number on roll of 89. By the following year, 1933, many improvements had been made. "Playground tar paved, partition erected in large room, gas lighting, central heating, water in girls' cloakroom, fences erected."

A History of Hatfield Heath

In 1938 through the initiative of the headmaster school meals were served for 45 children, being the first school in Essex to do so. Mrs Josie Smith of Blocks Farm was the cook using the poky scullery of the schoolhouse and a domestic gas stove. In wartime rationing conditions it enabled the children to have at least one substantial meal a day. Teaching staff supervised the meal for some years but eventually school meals service staff were employed to augment them. In September 11th 1944 we see, "School opened, meals now supplied from Hatfield Heath Cooking Depot."

The school had a number of names through the ages. From 1927 to 1932 it was "Hatfield Heath C of E." In 1932, it was "Hatfield Heath Council School" In 1933 it was changed to "Hatfield Broad Oak Heath Council School." All these were all age schools accepting children from 5 to 14 throughout. In November 1953 45 seniors transferred to Stansted Secondary Modern School leaving the Hatfield Heath School as "Hatfield Heath County Primary School."

In 1940 a kitchen was built next to the schoolhouse as a British Restaurant, a wartime move to serve the public. It was never used as such but reverted to a School Meals Service Central Kitchen. Miss Dorothy Search (when demobbed from the WAAFS) took over the task, serving up to 490 meals a day (at a cost of 5d a meal) for Hatfield Heath and eleven neighbouring schools. Two vans were stationed there with the dual purpose of delivering the food and transporting children who lived at a distance to and from school. This school meals service continued for 30 years until its closure in 1976.

During Mr Dix's time a large field adjacent to the school was acquired and made into the school playing field large enough for team games, football, cricket, rounders, sports and PT. Sometimes six or seven schools with all their pupils visited and competed at the Inter-School Sports.

1932 seems to have marked a great improvement in the school. In 1935 the HMI report was couched in the following terms; "Headmaster on excellent terms with his pupils ...... plays a very active part ...... out of school activities...... children behave well, speak clearly and enjoy their school life .... Infants good progress .... percussion and pipe band with bamboo pipes ...... a concert party ......" Yet in the same year they stated; "accommodation inadequate .... crowded."

By 1936 a school Penny Bank had opened and in 1938 HMI noted; "Hot lunches served ...... regular substantial, well prepared meals ...... great benefit." Police Officers were visiting the school in their "Road Safety" role, inspecting cycles and staging cycle tests.

The Schools

"1939 Sept. 18th. School reopened after the outbreak of war. Evacuees from Leyton, Clapton and other places have been billeted in the village. Owing to the large number of children the school is working in two sessions. The local children and private evacuees attend school in the morning and the government evacuees in the afternoon. Morning session 110 on register. Afternoon session 85 on register. Morning staff, Head plus 4 teachers. Afternoon staff, Head plus 7 Leyton teachers."

Mr Dix, as well as Headmaster, was also the Billeting Officer responsible for billeting all refugees in the village, a very difficult task indeed. The Men's Institute and Trinity Hall were pressed into service as extra accommodation. By August 1940 the numbers had shrunk to 146 of which 53 were evacuees and some of the Leyton teachers returned home. Realities of the war touched the school at the end of August 1940 and the entries in the school logbook illustrate this;

"Aug. 26th and Sept. 6th 13 Air Raid alarms in school hours, periods in shelter of 15 to 45 minutes.
Sept. 12th 60 Evacuees from Silvertown in Trinity Hall, children transferred to Men's Institute.
Oct. 17th & 18th School closed. Closure advised by police. Two unexploded landmines on Hatfield Heath side of Sheering.
Oct. 21st School reopened. Trinity Hall occupied by evacuees from Sheering. Infants accommodated in dining room at school. Air Raid alarm from 11a.m. to 1-15p.m. As children were not off premises until 1.30p.m. afternoon school cancelled.
Dec. 13th School closed for Delayed action bomb 100 yds from premises. 2 windows broken by another bomb which demolished house on opposite side of the road on previous evening.
Dec. 16th unexploded bomb, School closed.
Dec. 19th Bomb removed."

In 1941 the Mayor and Mayoress of Leyton visited the school. In June of that year "Miss Joan Halls commences a test as to her suitability for the teaching profession." In the same year five students from Hockerill Teachers' Training College started five weeks teaching practice at the school. This was the beginning of a connection which continued until the College closed some thirty years later.

The school meals arrangements were the focus of interest from other areas. Cambridgeshire's Domestic Subjects Organiser visited to see it working as did

A History of Hatfield Heath

other Essex schools' staff and heads. Foodstuffs being important in those beleaguered times once again farms looked to schools for help with labour. "School closed for pea-picking" appears together with "school closed for potato lifting."

In 1942 there was a visit from a Lieut. McDonald US Army, to talk about the USA. No doubt from one of the US Army Air Force bases in the district. A war time slant is given by the entries regarding the proceeds of school entertainments "£3-1-6 for the Red Cross Penny a Week Fund" "£2-10-0 for the Vicar's Forces Fund" "£9-17-0 for Salute the Soldier Week" and "£2-10-0 for Mrs Saville's Fund." Local needs were not forgotten however as we see that "Mrs Roberts sent 6d for each pupil at Christmas" a custom which stretched back to 1901 where we read of similar presentations being offered by Lord Rookwood. Later in the year the Welcome Home Fund had indeed a welcome addition, the proceeds of the school concert bringing in £17-10-0.

Accidents and illnesses occur with the same regularity over the years. "Amos Eton kicked by a horse .... hospital ... little hope of recovery" "Ray Mascall injured himself in head with billhook splitting wood without permission" "Alan Wilkinson had his fingers badly crushed in a lavatory door, Another boy was pushing the door to keep a third boy out" "Geofrey Perry swallowed a marble."

At last the welcome entry was made; "1945 May 8th VE Day, school closed."

As post-war life gradually resumed, stock was taken of schools nationally and it was found that education had suffered and was at low ebb. The impact of the movement of evacuees, shortage of teachers, large classes and run-down buildings showed in the reduced attainment level of many children. Progress and improvement depended on the hard work and dedication of the Head and teachers of the schools. Soon after the war a type of utility building called a HORSA. hut was built. It was used as a classroom and for morning assembly.

In 1945 25 seniors were transferred from Little Hallingbury bringing the numbers up to 139. The "New Dining Hall" was then used by the Infant class. When the number on roll rose to 160 at one period a mobile classroom was situated on the school field. Later, when numbers fell, it was removed. In March 1976 the "New Block" was built on the new "Open Plan" system with notional accommodation for four classes each of forty children. Although it was light and airy and had many useful areas it was not popular initially with teachers used to autonomy in a classroom away from others. This enabled the

The Schools

dark, cramped and unwholesome toilet block in the playground to be demolished leaving only inside toilets to be used. Also in the Post War period class outings ventured further afield; Kew Gardens, The Houses of Parliament, Regent's Park Zoo, Tower of London, the ballet Coppelia, Madam Tussaud's, Science Museum, Covent Garden Opera and even as far as Portsmouth and the Isle of Wight. Another innovation was Schools Radio which was introduced by the B.B.C. This was a great help to teachers as it acted as a foundation to many lessons. Singing, Nature, History, Geography, etc. for all children of school age. Essex County Council wired the whole school for radio from a master radio sited in the office. When T.V. for schools became available this too was introduced. The County Library played a part with termly visits by their library van supplying the school with 800 or 900 books on permanent loan, changeable on demand.

When Mr D Foster became Headmaster in 1956 the school had been a mixed Junior and Infant school since November 1953. It was staffed by a Head and three assistants; Mrs J Roberts, Miss H Dix and Miss Perry plus Clerical Assistant Miss Marler. The caretaker, Fred Bruty, shared duties with delivering meals to neighbouring schools. In addition there were two school meals staff, Mrs Hemmersley, Mrs. Saville and one other part-time cleaner, Mrs Bruty. The days of welfare and meals supervisors were yet to come. The Numbers on Roll, starting about 100, rose to a maximum of 160 in the seventies with children attending from outside the area. Indeed, at one time, the managers had to refuse admission to them on account of over-large classes. In 1956 the buildings were; Main School, Dining Room, Central Kitchen and lavatory block with flush toilets all adjoining the playing fields. Heating was by coke fuelled boilers with radiators. Essex County Council was known as a "good" Authority with generous per capita expenditure, permanent loans of library books, provision of clerical assistant and even summer camps for pupils. In the early 60s the furniture consisting of old oak dual desks was changed to light, modern desks or tables and chairs throughout. Children who had struggled to write using sharp steel pens and watery ink found it a great help when modern "Biro" type pens came in, freeing them from the blots and smears of yesteryear.

The days of a yearly, much feared, inspection were long gone. Ten years would pass between visits by Her Majesty's Inspectors. It was usual practice however for them to examine a school within a few years of a new Head being appointed. After two years HMIs came and spent a week in school, delivering their report on 3rd December 1957. A copy appears in the logbook and was quite complimentary: "..... Headmaster applied himself, with great energy, to the

A History of Hatfield Heath

organisation of the school ...... invigorating hand ...... children bring to school energy and high spirits ... lively and happy in their little community ...... broadcast lessons used ...... pupils contracted a positive attitude to their work and warm attachment to their school ...... sympathetic and encouraging start ...... Headmaster's whole hearted concern with all aspects of school life."

Although the foundation was no longer a Church of England school arrangements were made in 1956 for children to be withdrawn to attend Holy Trinity on three days a year for a child-run 40 minute service. It was still compulsory to hold a morning assembly for the whole school daily followed by Religious Instruction for each class as recommended in the "Agreed Syllabus" It gradually moved away from the usual hymn and prayer routine to a class presentation weekly with recorders leading the hymns and perhaps a short play. Parents began to attend, encouraging them to feel an important part of school life. This attitude eventually led to parents, especially of Infants, remaining to help with reading, always a problem with large classes.

The dreadful outbreaks of epidemics leading to school closures were, by now, a thing of the past, with improved health, sanitation and diet. Measles, mumps and other child illnesses were, of course, still prevalent but no longer feared or as lethal as in the past. Attendance remained steady at about 94% for over 25 years except for one day in 1958 when a blizzard closed all roads into the village stopping all buses causing some youngsters to have to walk home from Chelmsford after school, notably Richard Wilson, Anthony Foster and Robert Deards all ex Hatfield Heath County Primary School pupils then at the Grammar School.

Staff at the school remained settled over the years, which was a great advantage. Notable members were Joan Roberts (nee Halls), Kathleen Kilburn, Emily Payne, Mr Young and Miss Perry. Other long serving members of staff were Diane Barnett, Sheila Strutt, Brian Podbury and Jean Rostron, whilst in 1999 Doreen Pearson completed 24 years in the school meals service.

The all-age schools were coming to an end with the advent of the new Secondary Modern Schools at Stansted and Dunmow. At eleven the seniors departed to attend Grammar or Secondary Modern Schools leaving at 14, (later raised to 15), a selection examination deciding which school each child would attend. When Harlow New Town was built in the 1950s its new Comprehensive schools became available to Hatfield Heath. With no exam required, many parents opted for these as they offered a path to GCE exams, A Levels and further Education. The choice widened considerably. Thus in 1979 children transferred to schools as follows; Leventhorpe (Comp) 1, Waterside (Private) 1, Mountfitchet (Sec M) 8, Mark Hall (Comp) 9, Herts. and Essex (Girls High) 4, Margaret Dane (Comp Girls) 4, Bishop's Stortford Boy's High (Comp) 3, Newport Grammar 2, Passmores (Comp) 1, St. Mary's Convent (R.C.) 1. In addition to these Essex offered two boarding schools which some children from the school had attended in other years.

For many years the top juniors had had swimming lessons consisting of ten visits to the unheated open-air swimming pool in Bishop's Stortford. When the new swimming pool at Grange Paddocks opened pupils began to attend weekly for two terms a year enabling most children to swim with confidence by the time they left the school. In 1975 parents, lead by John Paine, Alison Watts, Margaret Lines and Val Richardson worked to build the above-ground learner pool on the premises, heated by North Sea gas. Open from April to October it proved so popular that, manned by volunteers, it opened at weekends and during the holidays. Costs for these, initially, were provided by Essex Education Committee but with the coming of cuts in the budget these payments ceased and schools were left to find their own resources.

An interesting departure from the usual junior syllabus was the teaching of French Conversation for a time. In the 70s audio-visual equipment was available to do this. A teacher, Mrs K Palmer, was engaged for mornings to take small groups from the top class. This was a valued introduction to French teaching in secondary schools. With the coming of cuts however Mrs Palmer's services had to be discontinued.

Sex education for children from the age of 8 was introduced, the BBC producing an audio-visual aid in the form of a filmstrip co-ordinated with an audiotape. Called "Where do babies come from?" it was available to parents before being shown in order that they might be prepared for any subsequent questions. This programme proved to be a success and continued yearly. After the initial showing one boy went home and said; "Yes, it was interesting, ... I think I will make it my hobby!"

One unusual activity was a sponsored litter picking drive with the twofold purpose of improving the aspect of the village and raising money for school funds. In 1979 pupils were sponsored by parents and friends to pick up litter by the hour. It raised a fair sum! This came to the attention of the "Keep Britain Tidy" group who were organising a competition between Local Authorities and others in connection with ideas to inculcate care of the environment. The school was chosen as one of the shortlist of 9 competitors invited to attend the

A History of Hatfield Heath

House of Commons to present their ideas. The other short-listed bodies were all local authorities viz: Darlington, Southall, Leeds, Berkshire, Isle of Man, Newton Abbot, Hartlepool and Derby City. All parties present had spent large sums promoting anti-litter awareness whereas HHCP School actually made money doing so. Donald Sinden, the well-known actor, judged submissions placing the school second after Derby City. Doctor Rhodes Boyson, (Education Minister) presenting a scroll to the two representative children Robin Douthwaite and Debbie Rand. The record of the four logbooks ends in Dec. 1981. On the first page of the last book is written:

" The Hatfield Heath Council School opens today in the building in which the church school has been carried on. The Staff is; Ralph Dix, Headmaster, Rose Elizabeth Emily May, Assistant, Florence E Waters, Assistant. April 4th 1932."

On the last day is written:

"Today I retire after 25 happy years here as Headmaster. It has been a happy and successful school of which I have been proud. I think that schoolmastering in general, and Headmaster of a small school in particular, such as this one, is the finest job in the world! I look forward with interest to its continuing success. Don Foster. Dec 18th. 1981."

The school has continued to flourish under successive heads and during 1994 embarked on a major rebuilding programme to provide a school for the village for the 21st century. The new building was opened on 4th April 1995 by Essex and England cricketer Mark Ilott.

HEAD TEACHERS

NATIONAL SCHOOL		BRITISH SCHOOL	
1866	Susan Barham (temp)	1857	Jane Aitkin
1866	Jane Babb	1872	Jane Palmer
1868	Elizabeth Furrell	1884	Miss Cooper
1872	Jane Turner	1885	Mr Spiller
1875	MA Nunn	1888	Mr JH Dixon
1878	Miss M Cooper	1891	Mr A Collar
1885	Miss Dalley	1892	Mr JE Carson
1886	Miss M Sharp	1895	Mr E. Rogers
1888	Mr EH Cates & Mrs Mary Cates	1921	Mr Ralph Dix
1893	Mr WH Keeble	1932	Joined with National School
1895	Mr Thomas Price & Mrs Price		
1899	Mr Montrose Stuart		

Move to new building

1900	Mr Charles Woodroffe Sharp
1903	Mr Montrose Stuart
1917	Mr WG Curtis
1926	Fan Sharman
1927	Rhoda Dix
1932	Mr Ralph Dix.
1956	Mr D Foster
1982	Mr D Jordan
1992	Mr D Walker
1993	Mr J Clements.

CHAIRMAN OF THE BOARD OF GOVERNORS

1932	Mrs Griffith
1968	Mrs M Hockley
1970	Mr F Delderfield
1983	Mr M Lemon
1997	Mr W McCarthy

A History of Hatfield Heath

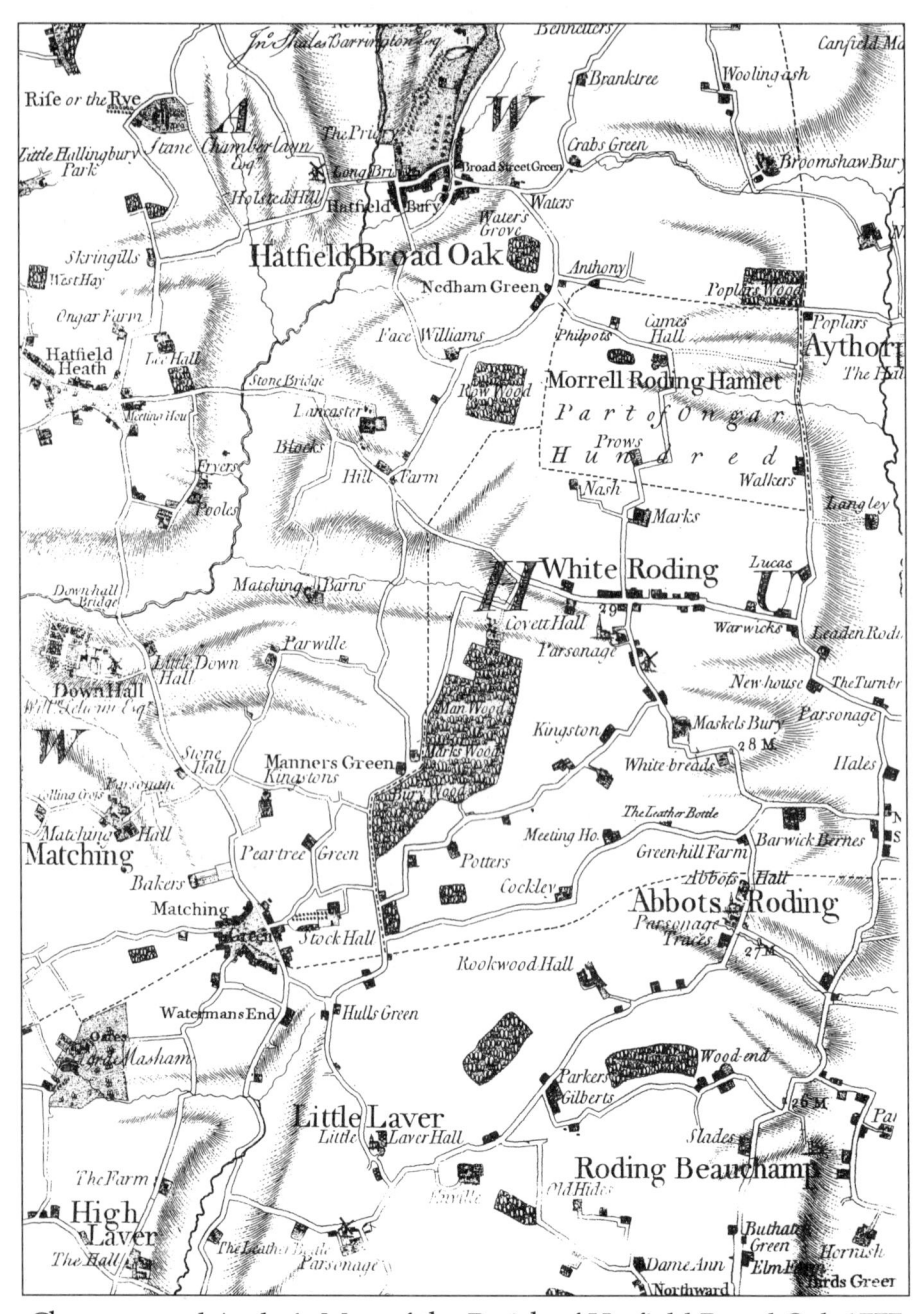

Chapman and Andre's Map of the Parish of Hatfield Broad Oak 1777

Daniel Day and 'Sudger' Newman watching a cricket match on the Heath, in the early 1930s.

Womens Institute garden meeting at Gladwyns in 1930.

The Hatfield Heath Brass Band displaying their trophies in 1946. Gilbert Hutchins, conductor, Ralph Dix, centre, Alfred Maskell, side drum, Alfred Jones, base drum.

JACK AND THE BEANSTALK 1975 ACT
"JACK"
Red velvet.
"GREEN FAIRY"
"DORA"
"SIMPLE SIMON"
COSTUME blue green white trousers
orange white blue shirt
"DAME" "MRS DURDEN"
4 "CHORUS" ADULTS
CHILDREN CHORUS
WEIGHT LIFTER
SOLDIER
CHARABELLE (COW)
U.V. BALLET.
JACK AND THE BEANSTALK 1975 ACT II
"ACROBAT" LUREX SUIT WHITE NET FRILLS.
"CHORUS"
3 ADULTS
PINK BLOUSE CORAL SKIRT.
YELLOW BLOUSE GREEN SKIRT.
"FORTUNE TELLER"
2. CHILDREN
BLUE DRESS
BLUE PANTS
BLUE MUFF
STRAW BOATER
2nd Girl in PINK

(IV)
The Twentieth Century

"Now nothing will ever be the same again"

Joseph Ashby Farmer & Countryman,
on hearing that the British ultimatum to
Germany had expired - 3rd August 1914.

At the start of the twentieth century the British felt secure in their island world for they had enjoyed a peaceful century at home. Abroad there had been many conflicts and during the past 20 years, a marked decline in their economic fortune, but Britain still saw itself as a race apart from Europe. The three indestructible forces the sea, the Fleet and the Empire would keep them safe and help boost a deep sense of national security and independence. Few could have thought to what extent these beliefs would be challenged, both in war and peace, during the coming century. It would bring about a new society, intent on self-improvement and, by the second half, a society that would be less divisive and more tolerant in its views.

In Hatfield Heath in 1900 there were two causes for celebration. Mr William Fowler opened the new National School on 1st August 1900, the Headmaster at that time being Mr CW Sharp. This building was designed to accommodate over 200 children and was built by local builder EH Hockley on land given by Sir Archer Houblon. The foundation stone had been laid on 28th September 1899 by the Very Rev. Montague Butler (grandfather of RA Butler Chancellor of the Exchequer in the post 2nd World War Conservative Government who was to be the architect of the new Education Act of 1944.) The old school, now called the Institute, was converted into a reading room, library and men's club and opened by Colonel Lockwood on 24th November 1900. A committee was formed to run the club which included Lord Rookwood, Horace Broke, the Vicar and twelve elected members from the village, Messrs. W Lewin, A Newman, W Bowyer, EH Hockley, AA Hockley, H Bretton, E Harris, D Day, S Sharpe, J Button, T Barker and Rev. Jude. Evening classes for adults covering various practical subjects were also run from here in 1902. The Parish Hall known as Trinity Hall had been opened in 1894 on land bought from Sir Archer Houblon by Lord Rookwood. These three institutions and their buildings would prove to be considerable assets to the village over the next 100 years.

Everyone on the Heath would have felt the death of Queen Victoria in 1901, for her reign had extended through most of her people's lifetime. Celebration of

A History of Hatfield Heath

King Edward VII's Coronation on 26th June 1902 was enjoyed by the entire village despite a severe rain storm midway through the proceedings. It started with a service on the Heath, then sports, a 'meat tea', more sports and finished with a bonfire and fireworks. Economically, however, there was little to celebrate. The Great Depression of 1873-1896 was still affecting agriculture with falling prices right up to the 1st World War, and Hatfield Heath was of course still very much an agricultural community. The gross national product from crop growing dropped from 20% in 1870 to just 6% by 1913 and this was reflected in the incomes of both farmers and farm workers. Early in this century the new Broad Oak Parish Council was expressing its concern to the County Council over the escalating rate for the poor. At Friars Farm around 1898, first William Alfred, then the other three older sons of John Hockley took advantage of the Government's Saskatchewan land purchase scheme and emigrated to Canada never to return. This left Albert the youngest son to continue farming at Friars upon his father John's death in 1909. It was in 1908 though that the State was able to introduce the first non-contributory Old Age Pension which went some way towards alleviating the conditions of the poor, as did the new Poor Law Act of 1909 and the National Insurance and National Health Insurance Acts of 1911.

The Heath lost one of its most generous benefactors in 1902 when Lord Rookwood (formerly Sir Henry Selwin-Ibbertson) of Down Hall died. His second wife Lady Eden, a great supporter of Matching Church and the Heath, who was wealthy in her own right, had died earlier in 1899. Lord Rookwood remarried in 1900, his third wife being Sophia Harriet Lawrell. Later in that decade, in 1909, Horace Broke of Gladwyns died. His son Col. Harry Broke had fought in the Boer war and returned in 1902 to play an important part in the village's life as did his sister Margaret (Mrs M Heathcote). Upon the sale of Barrington Hall in 1908 by the Lowndes family, Alfred Gosling became the new Lord of the Manor.

There were also some commercial upheavals in the village at this time. The brewery on the Stortford Road run by Gerald Bonham-Carter closed and was sold to the Edwards family to be converted into a flourmill around 1902. The Maltings at Gt Heath farm also closed down about this time. On the south side of the Heath adjacent to the cricket field Merchaws windmill ceased production in 1906 and was demolished in 1909. Mr George Buck started his store in 1912 from a cottage next to the White Horse. Alfred Little, landlord of the White Horse, bought a coal and coke depot in Mill Lane in 1905 from William Search before building Ivy cottage on this site in 1914. Near by, the Wagon and Horses, originally a barn and converted later to four cottages was changed from a simple beer house to a popular inn. At the west end of Post Office Cottages Mr CA Chapman sold newspapers to the villagers and passing trade and Ted Harris ran a cycle hire and repair shop. Mains water was available to some, supplied by the HBO Water Company.

The village held another Coronation celebration in 1911 with the crowning of King George V. A carnival procession was held around the Heath and sports and a tea organised by Colonel H Broke, J Button, EH Hockley the Rev. de Vere Watson and Rev. Jude among others. The world outside, however, was changing. The Government replaced 'Pax Britanica' with a new policy of 'Entente Cordiale'. From 1905, Britain, wary of Germany's growing power had entered into pacts with France, Belgium and Russia. Soon most European countries were signing protective alliances and the recipe for a mad and horrendous war was being created. A big page in world history was about to be turned.

Lord Grey's famous words of August 1914 were echoed locally when some of the oil lamps surrounding the Heath and lit faithfully by Daniel Day for so many years were taken down, never to be replaced. There were 79 volunteers from the village accepting the King's Shilling at the beginning of the war and by 1916, when conscription was introduced, more young men left for the front, the number under arms increasing to 149 by 1918. Only the older men, the infirm and those in reserved occupations were left. A local defence committee was set up under the chairmanship of John Balfour of Harlow with Mr AH Gosling and Mr C Gilbey the local representatives. Special constables were appointed under Ernest Hockley and emergency tasks allocated to the schoolmaster Montrose Stuart, the Vicars Rev. de Vere Watson and from 1915, the Rev. Edward Du Cane, as well as other villagers. As a 7 year old, Mrs Jessie Adams remembers her family being issued with instructions that in the case of an invasion they should prepare parcels of food, don warm clothes, carry blankets then follow the white arrows, pinned on posts and trees, into Hertfordshire! The routes chosen were on minor roads in order that military operations should not be hindered. Spare land was cultivated for vegetable growing and the vicarage used as a store for basic commodities. It is said that some young women from the village cycled each day to Braintree to work in the munitions factory.

The village was brought much closer to the war when AA guns were installed on the Heath and also when a Cyclist Company of the London Regiment under the command of Capt. Cole was billeted at Trinity Hall prior to going to Flanders. In 1916, a young Flying Officer from Farnborough, FO Prothero,

A History of Hatfield Heath

being completely lost, crashed his aircraft at Rolls Farm, home of Mr and Mrs Gus Reynolds, luckily he was unhurt. Later in the war Down Hall was brought into use as a military hospital. Bertie Woods was the war time village bobby having succeeded Arthur Trott, Thomas Charles, Henry Sutch and William Bridge. At that time the police house was located on the Sawbridgeworth Road on the left as you were leaving the village.

The war had upset the financial systems of Europe and this and the German U boat campaign inevitably brought about food shortages. By 1917 most foods were rationed including meat, bacon, cheese and tea. The Government brought in price guarantees and this greatly helped the plight of local farmers. At the same time the people were encouraged to save through the new National Savings scheme and certificates went on sale in the village.

Hatfield Heath first heard of the armistice in November 1918 when a gun crew from Sheering came through the village singing and shouting the good news. Both churches were filled for thanksgiving services and later victory sports were organised with a 'tea' set out on the Heath. The returning servicemen were warmly welcomed home, but there were 30 servicemen who did not come back. On 14th March 1920 Col. Harry Broke unveiled a memorial on the Heath to the men who had made the supreme sacrifice. For the first time the Great War had involved women in performing vital tasks in the war effort and this opportunity provided an important catalyst for a new, if somewhat slow, change in attitudes towards their roles in politics, business and society. They were able to reap some immediate reward for their labours when those aged 30 or over received the vote in the December 1918 'coupon' elections.

Britons however, although still remembering their dead, wanted to forget the war. The inter-war period was one of great expansion in travel. The train, charabanc, buses and, for the more affluent, the motor car and motorcycle brought people out of the towns and cities and into the countryside. Even the humble cycle played its part in introducing townsfolk to the Essex villages. The tradesmen of Hatfield Heath were to take full advantage of this situation. The four public houses, the Wagon & Horses, the White Horse, the Stag and the Fox & Hounds all played their part in providing refreshments to visitors and travellers. On the Chelmsford Road at Grand View, and across the road at Dunrobin, teashops were set up to catch passing trade. Later at Clipped Hedge Margaret Goddard had her own tea room facing the Dunmow Road. Mr & Mrs Matheson (Sophie Stone) had run the Fox & Hounds after the war and later Mr Filby, the new landlord, sold fish and chips from a hut in the pub garden. At Lea Hall Mr & Mrs Reynolds ran a guest house during the 1920s.

The Twentieth Century

Hatfield Heath's representatives on the Broad Oak Parish Council during the war and in the early twenties were EH Hockley, J Garton, J Button, H Bowyer, A Millbank, Col. H Broke and later, in 1925, Mr BTR Pyle and Mr G Buck were elected. Their main duties concerned the governorships of the three schools, appointment of overseers, the pricing and the upkeep of the water supply and of sanitation standards as well as the recommendations of repairs and new works to the Dunmow District Council whose parish representative was Mr Thomas Hawkey. At this time the polling station for elections was still at Hatfield Broad Oak and it was the duty of Charlie Sapsford to take voters from and to the Heath in his yellow wagon and pair. In November 1921 the Herts & Essex Water Company took over the business of the HBO Water Company. In 1919 recommendations for 8 houses to be erected on the Heath near Ongars and Peggerells were put forward and repeated in 1925, but no definite plans were acted upon until later in 1927 when 23 applications were received for the 8 homes. The Council was particularly concerned with fire fighting facilities as the old Merryweather horse-drawn fire tender, though excellently maintained by Mr WH Search, had by this time become well and truly outdated. An agreement was entered into with Sawbridgeworth Council for their brigade to attend fires in the parish with Bishop's Stortford's services as a standby. This measure proved to be very prudent as there were fires at cottages on the Heath, at Lancasters, Gibsons and Corringales farms, (where Farmer Millbank was ordered to pay the cost of £8-11s) and on a stormy night in 1923, lightning caught alight the thatched roof of the barn adjacent to the White Horse. Mr Ted Hockley summoned the brigade by bicycle as the telephone lines were out of action and those living nearby were forced to spend an uncomfortable night on the Heath. Unfortunately the barn was destroyed.

After the war the people of Hatfield Heath were learning to become less reliant on the fickle fortunes of farming. Friars farm bought their first tractor in 1919, an 'International', as the horse gradually gave way to mechanisation. The steam engine was a valuable source of power for ploughing, threshing corn and haulage duties. The government lifted the guaranteed agricultural subsidy in 1920 and prices fell, bringing the industry into another recession. Locally, however, the farmers turned to new products such as sugar beet, peas and potatoes. The sugar refinery at Felsted started to operate in 1925 and this encouraged the planting of beet. Mixed farming was also being undertaken with most farms keeping herds of cattle or sheep, pigs and poultry. Farms and fields became larger with Friars, Lancasters, Corringales, Shrubs, Ryes and Parvilles employing the majority of the farm workers. For years the great houses and farms had been the focal point of village life but mechanisation was changing the landscape from small fields to prairie acres and farmers needed less labour as they strove to become more efficient. The majority of the old Heath farms such as Ongars, Lea Hall, Heath (now Tudor Lodge), Little Heath, Hockleys (now Little Eden), Hill and Blocks were no longer farming in their own right and became private homes. In addition, those tenant farmers remaining took advantage of low prices and the death duties levied on the wealthy landowners and purchased the farms they worked. In 1920 Albert Hockley was to buy Friars and Pooles farms from St Bartholomew's Hospital for a sum of £4,500. This was the end of the hospital's ownership of Friars farm which had reached back over 600 years. Albert's son John was later to purchase land at Peggerells, Gibsons and Hill farms. From the great Down Estate sale of 24th June 1920 William Scantlebury purchased Parvilles farm of 393 acres, Mr A Douglas Pennant purchased Gibsons and Mr WP Bowyer bought Shrubbs. Lord Rookwood built the present farmhouse at Parvilles in 1900 near the original 17th century building which was destroyed by a fire in 1945. John Liddell acquired Peggerells farm in 1920 and later in 1927 James Liddell farmed Gladwyns before purchasing Shrubbs in 1950. Thus it was, that over the course of one thousand years the Great Estate of Hatfield, first owned by Edward the Confessor and Harold Godwin then William the Conqueror, followed by the Priory of Broad Oak and then by the great families of Barrington and Selwin – Ibbertson, was finally broken up into the smaller holdings we know today.

Despite the contraction in the agriculture industry other employment in the village was available. The Heath had several builders as employers, Ernest and Ted Hockley, Thomas Barker, the Trundle brothers Fred and Percy, Ted Smith of Mill Cottage, Frederick Barker of Manse Cottages and later Reg Search. Other local work was provided at Edwards' Mill, where Percy Clanford was manager for years, at Ernest Vale's implement business, at the three village butchers, the Stag garage run by Mr Charles Halls, Button's the harness makers and at Mills' shoe repairs. Further afield at Sawbridgeworth were Lawrence's joinery works, Taylor's Diamalt and the sack factory. In Bishop's Stortford Millars' Machinery, Priors instruments, the match factory, the expanding utilities and other shops and businesses also offered a variety of employment.

The social life of the village expanded too after the war. The football, cricket and snooker clubs all thrived and a tennis club with LC Stuart as secretary and J Robertson, treasurer, met on a court behind Trinity Hall. Whist drives were held on Monday evenings and Saturday dances in Trinity Hall where a band formed by Bill Bruty, Percy Day, Reg Day and Fred Slade frequently played. A 'black and white' minstrel group based at the Congregational Hall comprising Lily Day, Nelly Little, Olive Jackson, D Nichols, Herbert Maskell, Len Griffin,

Joyce Gray and Marion Gurnett provided local popular entertainment. Mr & Mrs Ralph Dix arranged excellent concerts, plays, socials and other seasonal celebrations. The cinemas at Sawbridgeworth and Bishop's Stortford (The Regent and the Phoenix) were also very popular.

In 1920 women were admitted to the Institute rooms and formed their own committee with Miss Stuart as secretary. This meeting was probably the forerunner of the village WI. During the war and most of the 1920s the vicar at Holy Trinity was the Rev. EA Du Cane probably one of the tallest clerics in the country at nearly 6' 7". He once overheard a small boy from the village enquire of his mother "which was the biggest - God, the Devil or the Rev. Du Cane?" In July 1924 the Hatfield Heath branch of the WI was formed with Mrs Carson as chairwoman, Mrs Cummins as secretary and Mrs Dix as treasurer. The Essex Hunt point to point races were held at Lea Hall on land owned by Col. Dalton White from 1931 to 1939. These meetings were moved to Matching Tye after the war. It was at the Lea Hall meeting in 1937 that the famous Warwick Vase ladies race was first run. Col. Dalton White persuaded the Countess of Warwick to allow a replica trophy of the Vase to be given in her name with the race to be run as an 'open' event for lady riders. Valerie Dalton White finished second in this pioneering event on *Laureate* and after the war her sister, Heather, won the Vase twice - in 1951 on *Piper Lad* and in 1952 on *Galician Gold*. An Ex-Serviceman's Association, with 69 members, was started in 1926 under the chairmanship of Capt. Powell with Mesdames Halls, French, Walden, Gunn, Barker, Dix and Day serving on the committee. This organisation became, in 1928, the local branch of the British Legion which soon reached a membership of 120 under the presidency of Col. Dalton White. A branch of the Ancient Order of Foresters met on the Heath and in 1927 a Sunday Afternoon Brotherhood was started with Sir Charles Bright, Col. Dalton White, EH Hockley, EE Hockley, E Lakey, N Cunningham, E Sapsford, W Smith, W Buck and P Newman prominent in its organisation.

The management of the Institute, which had been run by Holy Trinity from 1920 and the newly formed PCC from 1921, was handed back to a village representative committee in 1926 and shortly afterwards a lending library was started there. Hicks ran coaches to London each weekday and services to Bishop's Stortford were provided by Simpsons and Halls buses at a fare of 6d.

A scout troop under DH Buck was formed on the Heath in 1922. Mrs Ted (Lillian) Smith and later Kathleen Roberts and Phyllis Holcombe of Gt. Heath farm ran the Brownies troop. Miss Jude was the Girl Guides captain after the war. In 1925 she was succeeded by Miss Connie Pyle of Town Grove with Joan

A History of Hatfield Heath

Roberts as her lieutenant during and after the 2nd World War. In 1929 they won the Essex Guides Trophy and during 1930s held their summer camps at Fingringhoe on the Essex coast and at Golden Cap in Dorset. The Sunday Schools held an annual day out at Down Hall by kind permission of Lady Calverley and also ran outings to the seaside. Dorothy Search can recall the children of the village paddling in Pincey brook below Friars during hot summer days as a substitute for a seaside holiday. Between the wars it was customary for Heath families to take in 'Home Children' who came from very poor and usually large families. Harry King, a benefactor of the Heath, was one of these. Dorothy's mother would have two girls at a time staying, usually for about a year. Some 'mothers' such as Mrs Sid Day kept in touch with their former boarders over many years. The 5th November bonfire held on the Heath to the west of Holy Trinity was a major occasion for everyone, organised for many years by Ted Hockley and Manny Gunn. By the end of the 1920s the wireless was becoming an important factor in people's lives. The BBC had started to broadcast in 1922 and in the early days radios were run by accumulator batteries which could be charged up at J Button's shop and at the Stag garage by Charlie Halls and later by Eric Halls. Greenaways fair would visit the Heath once a year, originally on a site in Wagoner's Mead and later in a field on the Dunmow Road, just past Ongars. It should also be recorded that there was great rivalry in the 1920s and 30s between the Heath and Sheering villages both on and off the sporting field with many a fracas taking place in both villages, particularly at closing time!

Between the wars some well-known people lived in the village. Florence Desmond the actress resided at the Old Barn on the Dunmow Road as later did Nancy Henry a hand puppet expert. Sir Charles Bright who was the engineer responsible for the Atlantic cable installation lived at Little Brewers with his wife Isobel; earlier it was occupied by Mark Fisher the well-known artist. Sir Charles's daughter was to marry Sir Eric Berthoud the Ambassador to Poland who took up residence at Forbetts on the Bishop's Stortford Road and later at Gaston Green House and Major Horace Calverley, nephew of Lord Rookwood, inherited Down Hall, residing there until 1930. Capt. & Mrs Charles Gilbey bought Gibsons in 1931 while Hatfield Heath Grange in Sparrows Lane was the home of Rear Admiral Edward C Villiers, a famous seafaring name. The Broke family continued their long patronage of the Heath till well after the Second World War and organised many fetes in their grounds at Gladwyns. The late Col. H Broke's daughter Elizabeth was later to marry at Holy Trinity into the Boddington-Smart family who were famous for their climbing exploits.

The Twentieth Century

The 1930s saw a great variety of services provided in the village. The Stag ran a repair garage and petrol station and Jim Button, at the Beehive, sold ironmongery and similar products as well offering a taxi service. Mr Mills and Mr Frank Trundle repaired shoes on the south of the Heath, in the building where Footprint now stands, which was rented from Mr Henry Bowyer of the Laurels. Maud Harris ran the Post Office situated where the Chinese restaurant now trades. Later this shop was owned by Mr Peacock who in 1937 moved his shop to where the present Post Office is situated and where in the hairdressing dept. you could have a 'Marcel' wave for just 7/- (35p). Johnny Welsh and then Joe Smith were the Heath postmen at this time. Mr Buck sold groceries from his converted cottage stores and would cycle to Sawbridgeworth for the daily newspapers and to pick up any requests for supplies not stocked in his shop. A private lending library was operated from this shop between the wars. Brown Bros. ran their bakery on the Stortford road where Glasscocks still bake. Milk was delivered by Hockley's through Wally Brown and Fred Slade, and by Hallingbury Park farm. Milk could also be obtained from the Gt. Heath farm. Groceries were delivered weekly from Bishop's Stortford by the City and Home Counties store. Bill and Fred Bruty operated their coalyard on the south side of the Heath where, in April 1946, their thatched cottage was destroyed by a fire. This old residence, called Moat Cottages, had a recorded history from the mid 18th century but probably dated from much earlier, being part of the Barrington estate before being sold to a Mr Wilson in 1766. It was believed to have housed a Dame School around 1840 run by Mr & Mrs Dewbrey. Paddy Flack, 'Mutton Jeff 'and Tommy Beard from Sawbridgeworth were tinkers who travelled around the villages selling everyday items and mending pots and pans as they passed. Next to the Post Office Ted Harris still operated his cycle hire and repair shop, a feature on the Heath since about 1906. The Heath also supported three butchers; namely, Butlers (previously John Fowler), Reynolds and Cunningham. Dr White and then Dr Wilson ran surgeries from Hatfield Broad Oak, Drs Booth and Busby of Harlow and Drs Collins, Burton and Hailey from Sawbridgeworth also attended Heath residents. Mr Chamberlain was the school dentist. Thomas Claxton the village bobby later became the landlord of the White Horse. He was then followed by P.C. Woods, policeman during the Second World War.

There were several major events which occurred in Hatfield Heath between the wars and which still have an effect on the lives of villagers today. Some 34 acres of land known as 'back fields' and now accommodating the Broomfields development were sold by Hallingbury Place Estate to the Edwards family for £725 in 1923. Later this site was to become a gravel pit and part of it the village football pitch. The whole of the Houblon property at Hallingbury was put under the hammer during this period including the Estate clock designed by John Briant of Hertford and originally at Ryes manor house, plus a marble fire place purchased in auction and installed in Pompadours on the Chelmsford Road. Also put on to the market at this auction was the Hatfield Forest section of the Houblon estate which was eventually acquired by Edward North Buxton who clearly saw the need for its preservation. Upon his death in 1924 his sons offered it to the National Trust. Gas and water were laid on in the centre of the village in 1925 but mains electricity was still some ten years or more away. At Ardley End supplies were not connected until January 1953. Britain, after an excellent start given by Ferranti and Parsons was now falling behind the rest of Europe and America in the development of rural electricity supply.

In 1932 the two village schools, the Congregational 'British' School and the Church of England 'National' School amalgamated and became one school. The Essex County Council then took over its management as well as the responsibility for the building on a 99-year lease. It was in that year also that Down Hall became a girls' boarding school with Eleanor Howison Crauford as headmistress. The school closed in 1967. An important development in the provision of adult education facilities happened in 1929, when through the generosity of Mr BTR Pyle of Town Grove the Institute was extended to accommodate a larger library for villagers with Mr Ralph Dix as librarian. There was a grand opening ceremony performed by Capt. Cranham-Byng of Essex County Education Services and Col. Dalton White Chairman of the Trust. Mr Pyle was a director of Walter Lawrence's London building company, which also had a joinery factory at Sawbridgeworth and employed many local people including Mr Pyle's brother and his son Howard. Mr Pyle, who built Town Grove on the Dunmow Road in 1922, was also at this time the parish representative on the Dunmow District Council. Town Grove had its own bowling green, which was featured for many years in the Sutton seed catalogue. The Local Government Act of 1929 abolished the old Board of Guardians and transferred their function of the care of the poor to the County's authority. In 1933 the Lord of the Manor, Mr Alfred Gosling delegated the management of the Heath to the Parish Council and one of their continuing duties is to monitor any damage or encroachment. His son Mr CH Gosling succeeded Alfred in 1938.

It was due to the enterprise and generosity of Mr Pyle that the new houses at Bentley Villas were built in 1931 for the Dunmow District Council. This was followed in 1938 by the completion of the Ardley Crescent Estate and this enabled the condemned housing on the south of the Heath, near Footprint, called Davis Row, which had been subject to an inquiry in May 1936, finally to be demolished. Gouldens of Dunmow built both these new estates. Provision

The Twentieth Century

was also made on this site for playing fields, however this plan was never carried out. The population of Hatfield Heath in 1931 was 705, an increase from 645 in 1911 and 632 in 1921, a result of new developments in the village. Elm trees had lined the Chelmsford Road at this time but both here and on the Dunmow, Bishop's Stortford and Sawbridgeworth Roads there was a certain amount of private development and infilling both before the war and after. Some of these developments were able to benefit from the new main sewerage system laid on in the village centre in 1935 which was treated at a plant in the Matching road.

Daniel Day died in 1936 aged 82. He was a remarkable man who had joined the Army at 17, served in Afghanistan, India and S Africa and upon his return to the Heath served as sexton at Holy Trinity for over 47 years. He was a member of one of the old Hatfield Heath families who had lived here for many years and whose names keep recurring in these chapters. His father George Day was a great village character even when blind in his later years. Daniel's grandchildren are still in the area and have family connections with the Sapsfords, the Hockleys and the Rev. Herbert Brown. The Search and Gunn families also have had a long connection with the Heath. Harry Gunn born in 1871 was a steam engine driver and also drove hay carts to London. James Gunn worked the steam ploughs and lived with his wife Mary at Post Office cottages. James Search born in 1820 worked at Parvilles, his son Joseph, also a steam engine driver lived at Morley cottages and had 9 children. Percy Newman who took over from Charles Perry as village blacksmith had one daughter and four sons; Doris Henry, Charles, Stan, and Ted. Ted Newman worked in Buck's stores from before the World War II until the 1990s. There were other families whose names had a long association with the Heath, notably the Brutys, the Barkers, the Sapsfords, the Sylvesters, the Staines and the Mascalls (Maskells). The addition of surnames came into fashion in the 13th Century as the need arose for reliable identification. Many names have become corrupted over the centuries with different spellings of the original name.

The economic depression, which had been affecting everyone after 1920 and brought about a devaluation of the pound in 1931, eased in the farming industry after 1932 when the Government did a reversal on their previous policy and imposed foreign import quotas and tariffs. They also reintroduced grants for farmers and set up various marketing boards. From 1934 this protectionism boosted British industry at a time when its output was only half that of 1900 and helped give it some substance to meet the ordeals which lay ahead. However the village was able to celebrate the Jubilee of King George V in 1935 with a carnival procession and decorated floats. Two years later the

A History of Hatfield Heath

Coronation of King George VI was held on the 12th May 1937. There were Coronation spoons given to each child, and then sports on the Heath, followed by a carnival with decorated bicycles, vehicles and prams, a fancy dress parade, then tea and a grand finale bonfire with fireworks. But once again the storm clouds were gathering over Europe. The terms of the Treaty of Versailles of 1919 assisted the rise of Hitler and the Nazi Party of Germany in the 1930s, and once again this century the people of Britain would be asked to stand up for democracy and freedom. This time the front line would be on our very doorstep.

On the civil front, despite the passive view taken by some of those who remembered the carnage of the First World War, Britain was prepared for the conflict ahead. The wireless broadcasts of the 1930s kept the public well informed on necessary matters, and in 1939 upon the declaration of war with Germany Col. B Hoare of Colville Hall was appointed Local Defence Commander. P.C. Woods was the Heath's bobby during the war and Ralph Dix was Chairman of the Invasion Committee assisted by Mr Herald, Mr Buck run the ARP and organised a WVS unit operating from the Congregational Hall. Mr Gus Reynolds was in charge of the Home Guard, and Mr Ted Hockley kept the newly acquired trailer fire pump, a Merryweather 'Hatfield' appliance, at his yard and organised the fire watchers. In addition a YMCA centre was established in the Congregational Hall with the assistance of Mrs Buck, Mrs G Knight and Mrs Matheson, to cater for those far from their homes and families. Mrs Rob Firman and Ethel Franklin delivered Brown Brothers bread throughout the war while Mrs Fenner looked after the shop and Joe Smith and Florrie Rooke delivered the post. Signposts were taken down; iron railings and aluminium saucepans taken away for melting down to assist in the production of armaments. The vicarage garage was utilised as a salvage depot and its cellar became a cramped air raid shelter. Later, shelters were built at the top of the school playground. A gas attack indicator was erected on a pole in the village centre and one was obliged to look at this pole for any sign of potential danger as well as carrying a gas mask at all times. People were encouraged to keep chickens and to turn every available piece of land over to growing vegetables and fruit. At Mill Cottage the Guides tended allotments, growing potatoes for the war effort. The WI too played a leading roll in the village and operated fruit canning and preserving equipment in Trinity Hall. On one day a week 'Lord Woolton' pies could be brought from Bucks to eke out meals for, apart from bread, rationing had been imposed from 1940 on most foods, clothes and basic materials.

The Twentieth Century

In 1939 an influx of over 100 evacuees descended on the Heath and were billeted in the homes of many local families. As the phoney war progressed many returned home but appeared again after Dunkirk to stay for the duration, some indefinitely. Initially, schooling was provided for them in Trinity Hall, but later the village children attended the school in the morning and evacuees in the afternoon.

Over 100 men and women joined the services or left the village to perform vital war tasks and as a result were scattered throughout the world in the service of King and Country. Those who were left were in reserved occupations or trained in new jobs to ensure that the whole country made maximum use of its resources to meet the war effort. Many ladies including Heather and Valerie Dalton White, Mary Day, Sylvia and Pam Smith, Alice Gunn, Gladys Search, Kathleen Dix, Iris Coe, Georgina Richards, Phyllis Bentley, Grace Bogie, Helen Scott and Dorothy Search left the village to join the women's services. Some, including Nellie and Hilda Sapsford went to work in munitions factories. Other girls, including Peggy Austin, were employed away from the village or on the farms at Parvilles, Shrubbs and at Ryes. Danger, however, was everywhere and those working on the land remember having to take cover in any available ditch when air raids happened in daytime. During the Battle of Britain it was possible to get a good view of the dog fights taking place over the North Weald area from the south of the Heath and, because of its prominent position, it became necessary to camouflage the new houses at Ardley Crescent after a series of incendiary bombs had fallen. One night in 1943 Chelmsford was targeted for heavy bombing and Ted Hockley and his fire fighters spent that night and the next day assisting other brigades in clearing the damaged streets.

In 1939 Olive Mays, who had come to live in the village with her mother in 1924 and worked at the Stag, was given a 'crash' driving course in order to operate Charlie Halls' 20 seater Bedford coach and Austin Taxi on routes to Bishop's Stortford and Sawbridgeworth station, which she did throughout the war. As the war progressed Olive would ferry servicemen, Italian prisoners of war from the camp built in Mill lane, as well as the local doctor on his rounds and G Is on their nights out on the town. She was to run the gauntlet of bombs, bullets, shrapnel, drunken soldiers and airmen as well as suspicious policemen and the ever present ARP. You did not have to wear a uniform to play your part in this war. Petrol was strictly rationed and locally could only be obtained from Whalley's garage in Bishop's Stortford. Tyres came only from the Blue Star garage in Stansted Road. However, as proprietor of the Stag garage, Mr Charlie Halls was able to keep his coach and taxis in good repair.

A History of Hatfield Heath

Bridge, whist drives and weekly dances were held in Trinity Hall where with the help of the WI, money was raised for such causes as 'Warship Week', 'Spitfire Week', 'War Weapons Week' and the 'mile of pennies' placed along the road in front of the Post Office. Mrs Berthould and the Rev. Gardiner ran youth clubs for both village children and evacuees and Rhoda Dix formed a country-dancing group held in Trinity Hall. From the Institute Robin Whitbread and Gilbert Hutchin organised and taught the village youth brass band and in July 1945 they were to achieve success in the London and Home Counties band competition. One peculiarity of this time was an Eisteddfod held on the Heath for four consecutive years from 1943 to 1946. National Savings certificates were being promoted everywhere with savings collectors in every road. Beer, although rationed, always seemed to be available at the four pubs in the village and at organised functions. At Gibsons, Capt. Charles Gilbey a director of the P&O Lines stored many of the Company's ships' fixtures and fittings in his barns and Mr Childs moved his glass factory away from the blitz in Leyton to a safer haven at Gt. Heath Farm where it remained until the 1950s. In January 1942 the churches organised a National Day of Prayer and this was continued throughout the war on a monthly basis.

Locally there was a huge increase in the war effort during the later part of 1942 and into 1943. The Americans had entered the war and their engineers were building new airfields at Stansted, Matching, Wethersfield, Willingale and Easton Lodge. In addition there were British air bases at North Weald, Hunsdon, Debden and Sawbridgeworth. A new prisoner of war camp was built in Mill Lane in 1941/2 and the occupants were put to work on the farms and to maintaining ditches and streams. For the next two to three years the parish would experience a huge influx of foreign personnel; American engineers and airmen, Free French and Poles, and Italian and German prisoners, as well as our own servicemen and the evacuees from London. The village at this time took on a very cosmopolitan feel to those local residents trying to provide hospitality and comforts to those far from their homes. Some German and Italian prisoners remained here until 1947 and one, Werner Hoffman, a brilliant musician, had been organist at Cologne Cathedral before the war. At least one Italian family too came to settle in the district after the end of hostilities.

This increased activity inevitably attracted the German bombers and on 13th December 1940 the Churchgate House on the Heath just north of the Institute was completely destroyed by a large bomb. Fortunately the occupiers Nurse Freeman and Mr & Mrs Roly Bayford and family were not at home at the time. Several incendiary bombs landed in the village during the war and a 500lb bomb created a 65ft wide, 15ft deep hole in the cricket field in June 1944 while another landed on the east side of the Heath near the Malt House. An enemy Dornier bomber crashed near Down Hall and one member of the crew was killed while another was taken prisoner in Manwood. The deadly land mines as well as V1 rockets also fell about the district in 1943 and 1944 causing much damage. In September 1944 a tragic accident happened in the village when a USA Airforce B26 Marauder trying to find its way back to its base at Matching in bad weather crashed on the Chelmsford Road, not far from the Congregational Church, killing the crew and destroying the houses occupied by Mr Brown, Mr Mills and Mrs Ivy Little. Fortunately no local people were hurt. Another American bomber flying out of Stansted and heavily laden came down in Mr Robart's field to the west of the Sawbridgeworth Road killing all the crew. With the D-Day landings in June 1944, however, the tide of war turned in favour of the allies and the aerial danger diminished.

On 8th. May 1945, VE Day, the village celebrated all day. The RAF Sawbridgeworth descended on the Heath and everyone drank and danced until the early hours with a large bonfire being lit on the east side of the Heath. A celebration dinner and dance was held on 29th May in Trinity Hall and the village prepared for the service men and women to come home. However 17 men from the village had given their lives for their country and did not return. A Welcome Home fund was set up early in 1945 and this fund paid for a VJ dance and a grand dinner held on 12th February 1946, as well as cash for service personnel and their widows. The Institute's west wall and the Chelmsford Road bungalows were repaired while the cricket pitch and other scars of war made good. The returning service personnel brought with them their husbands and wives, girlfriends and boyfriends and the Heath would no longer be the parochial village of the past but a much more outward looking society. The National and Local Governments were therefore required to plan for both old and new villagers with regard to housing, schools, work and social needs.

There was a groundswell of feeling among the public in 1945 for a new beginning to the way that their lives should be governed after the devastation of a Second World War. The conflict had left Britain bereft of wealth, no longer a superpower, having to sell off its overseas assets and to plan its economy without the support of the Dominions, who were intent on gaining their independence. The country was endeavouring to repair its confidence and become a more humane and democratic society. It benefited from the Marshall Aid Plan whereby the USA provided capital items to enable Western Europe to regain its full production capacities. During the war the Americans had devised the scheme of lease-lend and this had given local farmers the

A History of Hatfield Heath

opportunity to acquire the very latest agricultural machinery available. A self propelled combine harvester operated at Parvilles under this scheme early in the war. Parliament too was not to be deterred by the problems arising from the War and as early as 1944 had passed a new Education Act and had agreed at the Bretton Woods Conference to join in setting up a monetary fund under the control of a World Bank. The Beveridge Report of 1942 resulted in the birth of the National Health Service in 1948 and National Insurance and Family Allowance Acts came into force in 1946. The New Towns Act of 1946 was framed to provide much needed housing with Harlow chosen as one of these developments. Britain, however, was in a period of great austerity, bread rationing had started in 1946, and the new slogan " Export or Die", required priority for our goods and services to be sold abroad. The western world entered a period known as the 'cold war' with its neighbours in the east, the Communist bloc, and this led to a feeling of great apprehension concerning the atom bomb and the spread of nuclear conflict. To make matters worse the winter of 1947 brought in very severe weather, causing considerable hardship on the Heath and throughout the country.

Locally the village was echoing the national mood in its efforts to rebuild after the war. The Parish Council was divided into three wards, the Heath representatives being BTR Pyle (chairman), Margaret Goddard, Mssrs R Bloxsome, R Dix and E E Hockley; the last two gentlemen later served as chairmen. In 1947 the Council expressed great concern over the dangerous junction where the Harlow Road met the Chelmsford and Broad Oak Roads and also at the speed at which the German ex-POWs were driving through the village past the school. Their practice of taking up most of the spaces on the Saturday bus service to Bishop's Stortford was also noted and passed on to the Eastern National Bus Co. The Harlow junction was much later redesigned to its current configuration. In 1946 plans were made by Mr Pyle for new accommodation in the village with an estate of 38 houses on 'back fields' to be called Broomfields. Reorganisation of the local schools and their canteen facilities through the 1944 Act were implemented with some twelve schools being catered for in the Hatfield Heath kitchen. The National Heath Act in turn was to change the provision of medical services. From 1958 Dr Bennison held his surgery at Hatfield Broad Oak in the old Cottage Hospital and initially held a surgery at the home of Len Griffin overlooking the Heath and also at Clipped Hedge. By 1960, a van was used for consultancy visits to the Institute, but a purpose built new surgery on the Heath was not opened until 1969.

A Village Hall Trust Fund was started in 1947 with Mr J Herald as president, Mr DH Banner secretary and Mrs Herald treasurer. The money for this came

The Twentieth Century

from the remains of the Welcome Home balance, plus compensation received for damage to the Institute wall together with a generous donation of £500 from Mr BTR Pyle, who died in 1952. Later this initial fund was enlarged by profits from church and village fetes held at Bentleys, Lea Hall and Gladwyns as well as other local funding. It was also at this time that the management of Trinity Hall reverted to the PCC This old hall was given a new floor partly through the generosity of Mr Strickland-Skailes of Lea Hall, then redecorated and an extension built on the rear. The long awaited new housing estate at Broomfields (back fields) was started in 1948 on land purchased from the Edwards family and was built by Messrs Helmer & Dyer. The first tenants were handed their keys in March 1949. This estate was extended in 1954 and 1955 by another 24 homes built by Butlers of Dunmow. These developments provided much needed housing for the people of Hatfield Heath but were subjected to some controversy in their early stages. The site was a reclaimed sandpit and in order to gain access it had been necessary to demolish four of the properties at Morley cottages, homes of Mrs Trofinor, Mrs Flack, Florrie Rooke and Mrs Layfield. The District Council also looked into the possibility of converting the prison camp for residential housing and considerable correspondence between the Department of Housing, the Ministry of Defence and the Council took place, in the end to no avail as the project was deemed to be too expensive. This site, originally owned by Richard Staines of Lt. Heath farm, and then by Richard (Dick) Dean was later utilised by John Fish for his Greenway's egg packing company. It was also at this time that the first housing in Harlow New Town was being occupied and the industrial site developed in 1951 in Edinburgh Way provided much welcomed diversity of employment for local people. Planning permission was granted to the Essex Constabulary in November 1954 to build a new police station on the Chelmsford Road, which involved the redirection of a public footpath, and this was completed in 1956. P. C. English and P. C. Potter were the first residents, followed by Sgt. Llewellen and 'Jock' Reid. Later, in the 1960s, Sgt. Calver and P. C. Smith were the village bobbies.

Frank Gates the Ford dealer lived at Lyndhurst on the Matching Road and had family connections with a commercial development at Matching airfield involving the production of fabricated concrete parts, which employed several village people. Mr Gates daughter, Marjory Mealing, still lives in the village at Heath Lodge. At Clipped Hedge where Margaret Goddard had run her tea room, her son John Goddard, with the assistance of Geoff Smith, started a turkey farm after the war employing several local people including Gilbert Hutchin, Lyndon Long, and Malcolm Jackson. There were three nursery/ market garden businesses on the Heath during and after the war, one run by

A History of Hatfield Heath

Mr Bertschinger on the Sheering Road another by Alf Patmore, Mr Jenning and then Mr Kent on the Sawbridgeworth Road and one by Mr Caton at Tudor Lodge. All had closed by 1973. Mr Child's Glass works at Great Heath farm which had employed several villagers including Sid Collins, 'Brusher' Wilson and Alfred Adams was, however, not allowed to expand and eventually moved to Bishop's Stortford. In 1951 this site was subject to an application for a petrol filling station. As a boy in the late 1950s and early 1960s the present Poet Laureate Andrew Motion lived with his family at Little Brewers in Mill Lane. Another local person of interest was Miss Bear granddaughter of Walter Witham owner of the Laurels and the Beehive in the 2nd half of the 19th century. Miss Bear, who was lame, lived at Mill View on the Bishop's Stortford Road and was often seen around the village in her hand propelled tricycle.

Farming was to receive a boost by the 1947 Agricultural Act which guaranteed prices and later set up marketing schemes for milk, eggs, cheese, fatstock and some vegetables. This Act also gave a greater security of tenure to tenant farmers who previously could be asked to vacate their farms with less than one year's notice. Since the beginning of the war there had been a tremendous increase in land under plough from 12 million to 18 million acres, this was coupled with a much higher output per acre. The farmers of Hatfield Heath, now only some seven in number, needed to reinvest their profits into more and more advanced mechanical equipment in order to remain competitive. In 1957 there was a large fire at Gladwyns when the barn, its new drying equipment and the newly harvested corn were destroyed.

The mass-produced motor car in the 1950s enabled local people to travel farther in search of employment. In addition the greater availability of consumer products, including the TV set, considerably changed their habits. The public adored the cinema and its stars and the radio attracted huge audiences, but now television was appearing in the home and would challenge the more traditional forms of entertainment available. Olive Mays was spending more of her time, along with Eric Halls, driving Halls' coaches after the regular driver William Skinner was killed in a road accident near the Mill on the Bishop's Stortford Road. She completed 36 years as a PSV driver and became a popular ambassador for the village, driving her bus all over the country. Ernie Rickards was also a well known Halls driver at this time. The Festival of Britain in 1951 was both a celebration and shop window in displaying the skills of the British people to the rest of the world and many from the village made the trip to London and the South Bank site. On June 2nd 1953 the village celebrated the Coronation of Her Majesty Queen Elizabeth ll. Despite the excellent organisation the weather was appalling. The village sports were delayed and the Carnival procession postponed until the evening.

The Twentieth Century

The day finished with fireworks and a bonfire, then a choice of Whist Drive in the Institute or a Dance in Trinity Hall, both starting at 10 pm! At the dance, presentations were made to Mr A Bruty and Mr H Bruty for their long service on behalf of the Cricket Club and to Mr H Pyle of the Football Club, which had won two championship cups that season.

It was due to the efforts of Cmdr. Reay Parkinson that in 1963 The Hatfield Heath Association was formed with the object of providing local amenities, protecting the nature of the Heath and fostering a sense of community within the village. Mr Cakebread and then Peter Lines were the chairmen and Mr Stewart and later Cyril Claydon were the secretaries, with Leonard Faint as treasurer. Other committee members included Beryl Aves, Herbert Maskell, Mr & Mrs Bennett, Mr & Mrs Delderfield, Don Foster, Mrs Frith, Mrs Diana White of Ongers, Mr Woodhouse of Gladwyns, Mr & Mrs Burlingham, Geoff Smith, Alan Wilkinson and Sgt. Calver. Plans had been laid in the mid 1960s for the M11 motorway and Heath residents had expressed concern that an intersection at Sheering would involve a huge increase in traffic in the village. The Association played a part in stopping this particular plan with a petition organised by Beryl Aves and Cyril Claydon. The Harlow to Bishop's Stortford section of the motorway was finally opened on 23rd July 1975 without the Sheering intersection. This organisation survived some three decades, latterly as the Villagers Association with Colin Skyrme and then Ken Bennison as Chairman, Jean Clarke secretary and Rob Jones treasurer, but is now defunct. Cmdr. Parkinson was also responsible for the creation of a boys' club in the village and a gymnasium and boxing ring were set up in his barn at Corringales, while sailing, outings to places of interest and adventure were organised. Tours were also made to Denmark and to Iceland.

The early 1960s was a period of great expansion and most people felt they were at last better off after the austerity of the earlier decade. By 1958 the whole village had been supplied with electricity and for the first time in its recorded history Hatfield Heath was no longer a mainly agricultural community. The Heath based farms now consisted of John Hockley at Friars, Wallis Scantlebury at Parvilles, John Garton of Ryes, John Liddell of Shrubs, the Couch and Hunt families from Lancasters, together with Capt. R Bloxome of Peggerells and the Robarts from Stone Hall on the Hallingbury Road, a huge decline from the 40 farms of 1700. The Heath's representatives on the Parish Council at this time were EE Hockley, R Dix, RE Bloxsome, WA Bruty and J Garton, and later H Pyle and Mrs Beryl Aves. While Mrs Dearlove was the District Councillor. The first draft of a village plan envisaging 120 new homes was produced in 1961 and this was partly realised in 1962 with the building of the Cox Ley extension by

A History of Hatfield Heath

Morgans who also gave the land which is now the village hall car park and access road. By 1961 the population of Hatfield Heath had reached 1000 and most people were commuting to work. Further developments occurred again in 1963/4 when local builder Peter Brown built the Little Heath estate and later in 1966/7 he completed the Clipped Hedge development. About this time too Peachey & Peachey built Wagon Mead. Other smaller developments took place in the village as new people took up residence so that by the 1971 census the population had dramatically increased to 1531. As a result of a 1965 Act the Heath no longer held the status of a common and it was later registered by the Council as a village green. For the first time in centuries no animals grazed the Heath, the rights of which were confined to just one or two houses.

Within Hatfield Heath too there were some important commercial changes. Mr and Mrs Lockley had taken over the running of the Post Office from the Peacocks in 1962, after a brief period of occupation by Mr Harris. On the Lockley's retirement the business was run by Mr Wickenson who also kept the White Horse and Bucks Stores. The business of JJ Button at the Beehive closed for good in 1961 and Mr Button moved to Bishop's Stortford. The Mill on the Stortford Road also closed in the early 1960's and was purchased by Mr Sid Jackson for use as a warehouse; later this building became a manufacturing unit of M&D Lighting. Ted Hockley sold the family's long-standing building firm and its yard to Mr Sargeant's Sarbir company in 1966. This company has since become a steadfast employer and supporter of the village. At this time too the Wagon and Horses was extended and the garage at the east of the Heath, Whites was expanded to cater for the increase in car ownership. Mr Frith, then Mr Roberts, who had run the Downham girls' boarding school, and later Mr & Mrs Ormerod owned this garage. In 1935, Albert White had a poultry farm on the Chelmsford Road and from 1945 was operating a taxi service. More recently his son John has run a motor engineering business there. John is known in the region for his involvement in auto and rally cross, first driving his Mini-Cooper and more recently as an administrator. Mr & Mrs C Tayler opened a petrol station in 1966 on the site of the Gt. Heath farm and later the restaurant 'Hunters Meet' was added.

The winter of 1962/3 was one of the worst on record with the whole village frozen up from December until the following March, causing severe disruption to travel, building work and sport as well as bringing great hardship to the elderly. However, Arthur Wilkinson, the highly regarded village milkman, managed to complete most of his rounds, indeed by the time of his retirement he had served the village for 48 years only interrupted by his war service.

The Twentieth Century

The economic benefits achieved in the first part of the decade were short lived as Britain underwent a period of industrial decline in the late 1960s being outperformed by most other European countries and this in turn led to a period of high inflation. The Government was forced to change its policy on subsidies for the farming industry and people had to pay more for their food in line with the Europe's Common Market policy. This strategy eventually benefited local farmers but it also bought about a decline in the country's general standard of living which lasting for several years. It was partly due to the benefits of North Sea gas and oil, which started to flow in 1975 that a higher standard of living was enjoyed in the final part of the 20th Century.

The prosperity of the early 1960s led to new facilities being made available on the Heath and in 1966 a new cricket pavilion was built after much planning and hard work by Mr H Pyle and the committee which included S Barker, D Search, F Bruty, J Brown, R Nicholls, S Turner, D Chapman, Dorothy Search and other members. The pavilion was also used for fund raising bingo nights run by Mr Herbert Maskell and Toffee Turner. Cmdr. Parkinson formed an ad-hoc committee in 1966 with George Brown, Don Foster, Geoff Smith, Leonard Faint, Cyril Hackett and others to endeavour to get the project of a new village hall off the ground. In 1968 Trinity Hall was again leased from the PCC to the Village Hall Trust for a period of 56 years at a peppercorn rent of 1/- (5p) per annum and plans were then made to built a new hall on the site. Trinity Hall, looked after for many years by Jim Button with Arthur Kent the caretaker, was now showing its age. Finance for the new hall was provided from various funds, some of which had been started as far back as 1947 with the remains of the Welcome Home funds. Because of the shortage of building materials after the war, the Parish Council invested these funds until they were required. However controversy arose in 1968 when the parish of Hatfield Broad Oak as a whole voted in a poll that the Council should not provide any public finance towards this project. Views had been expressed as early as 1962 for the two parishes to split and although relationships between councillors had always been good this event would go further to foster this opinion. In the matter of raising new hall finance the Heath was now on its own. Roland and Ruby Hole organised old-time dances and the committee ran other fund raising activities including jumble sales and garden parties. Cyril and Alice Hackett ran a monthly '100' club draw with some 250 members. In 1967 and 1968 fetes were held at Mr & Mrs Burlingham's home on the Sawbridgeworth Road, a forerunner of the Hatfield Heath Festival. However it was apparent that building costs were escalating faster than income and the chairman Don Foster put it to the committee that a much larger fund raising event which would attract crowds from outside, was needed. A Hatfield Heath Midsummer

A History of Hatfield Heath

Festival was born and held for the first time on 20th June 1969. Events included a Ball and Dinner at Down Hall organised by Kay Vartan, dance groups, an Arts and Crafts Exhibition run by Irene Delderfield, a musical concert and a quiz plus a museum of bygones and costumes organised by Cmdr. Parkinson and Jean Foster, which was held at the Beehive. Moot House Players performed a play in the squash court of Lea Hall and Humphrey Littleton and his jazz band gave a concert in a circus sized marquee on the school playing fields, which had been organised by police sergeant Alan Ashworth. The festival was supported by a refreshment marquee run by Cyril and Alice Hackett, stalls, flower exhibitions in both churches, and a challenge quiz with other local villages. A creditable profit of £850 was realised.

A Government grant of £7000 was received in 1969 towards the cost of the hall, and in addition, a 'Village Hall Notes' scheme was introduced by Roland Hole in which villagers were able to make loans to the trust on generous terms. This raised £1800 repaid to donors over three years. Therefore, with the amounts raised through grants, loans and by efforts of the people of Hatfield Heath, the Trust was able to accept a tender of £13500 from Peter Brown to erect the new hall, the architect being Peter Ball. Trinity Hall was demolished in September 1969 and the new hall opened officially on 28th March 1970 and celebrated with 5 year old Robert Barsted and 80 year old Beatrice Sapsford cutting the tape. A celebration dinner and dance was held on 4th April with speeches made by Cyril Hackett chairman of the Building Committee, Don Foster chairman of the Trust, Cyril Claydon secretary to the Trust, Cmdr. Reay Parkinson former chairman, PW Gee, solicitor and for the guests Brig. CGC Wade Deputy Lord Lieutenant of Essex. Peter Lines was an original member of the building committee and together with Margaret Lines, Joe Liddell and later Diane Taylor, Peter Noel, Geoff Smith and Alan Wilkinson have completed more than 30 years association with the Hall and the Festival. George Brown and Mrs Claydon were also long serving committee members from the embryo days of the new hall. The popular Harry Crome was the first village hall caretaker and he was then succeeded by Bill Pleasance. Later Country and Western dances were run by Geoff Larke, Alan Wilkinson and Pete Campen which contributed considerably to hall funds In the small committee room were placed an aerial view of the Heath donated by Mrs Burlingham together with two-watercolour paintings previously donated by the Rev. W Allen in 1935 to Trinity Hall. In the late 1950s a dispute had arisen regarding the ownership of the Institute as it was claimed to have been built on consecrated ground. This matter was never resolved to everyone's satisfaction and despite sterling work done earlier by the Rev. Ronald Smythe and Arthur Prescott when the building was leased to the village youth club, the fabric of the building was by then in dire need of attention. Therefore in 1974 an agreement was signed by the PCC and the Village Hall Trust putting the Institute under a similar arrangement as that of the Village Hall for a period of 49 years and the much needed renovation work was then undertaken by the Village Hall Committee. Mr Strickland Skailes performed the grand reopening on 3rd September 1977.

The initial success of the Midsummer Festival was continued in the 1970s with most of the village taking some part in this annual fund raising exercise. The highlight was always the parade of village children organised by Joy Passfield, Wendy Bundy, Kath White and Diane Taylor with a different pageant theme chosen each year. During the last 30 years a considerable sum of money was raised from the Festival for the upkeep of the two halls and for the benefit of other Heath organisations in terms of grants and preferential hire rates. Hatfield Heath can be proud in the efforts made by so many people, too many to mention here, who came from all walks of life, and who gave their time, energy and cash in the successful completion of these projects and also in the work undertaken for the maintenance of their continuous use. On a sad note it has to be to recorded that after 30 successful years the Hatfield Heath Festival was not held in 1999. Both the Village Hall Trust Management and Executive Committees members have, over these 30 years, given a considerable amount of time and effort to ensure the two halls were available for use by village organisations and village residents. Mark Lemon was the Trust chairman during the 1980s & early 90s and former secretary Mike Briscoe is the current chairman with Keith Fox secretary and Ian Kettridge treasurer. In 1999 an agreement between the Trust and the PCC led to both parties providing finance to renovate the Institute kitchen and main hall interior. An enthusiastic team led by Mike Cargo carried out the work and once again this old building is ready to serve the community in the years ahead.

In 1971 the old Parish Magazine, first published in 1893, became the Village Magazine and appeared in 1972 with a new modern cover. Editors were jointly, John Paine, Tony Bushell and the Rev. Ronald Smythe with Wendy Bundy as secretary and 'Beaker' Burlingham treasurer. Later editors were Jill Errington, Janet Briscoe and Kingsley James. Jean Clarke was, for many years, responsible for distribution now undertaken by Olly Jones. Tony and Barbara Jenkins as chairman and secretary had a long association with the Magazine and the current editor is Breda May.

In 1975 Connie Pyle celebrated 50 years association with the Girl Guides at Hatfield Heath. The village was also able to celebrate the Queen's jubilee in

A History of Hatfield Heath

1978 with a fete and sports together with a local history exhibition in the cricket pavilion organised by Cmdr. Reay Parkinson. In 1979 the village was able to welcome the Right Honourable Patrick Jenkin who came to live at Home Farm near Down Hall. Mr Jenkin served in Mrs Thatcher's Cabinet as Secretary of State for Social Services in 1979 and later as Industry and the Environment Minister as well as holding other posts. He was created Lord Jenkin of Roding in 1987. The Hatfield Heath ward of the Parish Council was represented by Don Foster, David Tyler, Olive Mays, Margaret Lines, Howard Pyle, Beryl Aves and Bill Bruty.

There were further commercial changes in the village in 1973 when the Post Office was acquired by Mr & Mrs Barry Rand. Bucks Stores also had a new series of owners and new trading names. In 1970 a cottage at the end of Post Office row was converted to become the Coffee Pot, the old Post Office, after some time as a greengrocers, opened as a Chinese restaurant. In 1975 Mr F Trundle retired from his shoe repair shop after 48 years, the premises were then taken over by the Footprint business. The old established butchers businesses of Reynolds and Taylers both closed in the 1990s, the buildings both at Pond Lane and adjacent to the Stag became small groups of shops. Mr CH Gosling the Lord of the Manor had died in 1974 and in 1977 Barrington Hall was sold first to British Livestock and then, in 1980, to Contemporary Perfumes. Mr Rupert Gosling succeeded as Lord of the Manor, the Heath now being owned by the Gosling Trust. In 1988 Heather Whitfield and Pamela Corbitt acquired the Post Office business and Bucks Stores also changed ownership under Barry Pinder. In the following year 1989 Mr and Mrs Taylor relinquished Hunters Meet restaurant which has, since 1990, been run by Mr Brendan Carrig. The Countryman also had a new owner and the garage on the south of the Heath owned by Mr & Mrs Omeroyd became Heath Engineering. The abattoir business of Church & McLaren closed in 1987 and site was later developed as The Shaw Estate and the village car park. In 1996, the village stores was acquired by the chain store Alldays and the Coffee Pot became a Chinese take-away. Doctors John and Kathleen Bennison ran a practice in the village for many years and were joined in 1976 by Dr Ian Gilchrist. Ten years later when the Bennisons retired Drs Peter and Katherine Orton joined the practice. The new medical centre was then built on the existing site in 1990. A new system of rural policing was set up by the Essex Constabulary in the mid 1990s and this came into effect in Uttlesford in 1999 when the Hatfield Heath station became one of four areas within the District to be used as an operating centre and the building was extensively modified.

The Twentieth Century

The new Hatfield Heath Parish Council was elected in 1987 and met for the first time on 1st April under the chairmanship of Mr Don Foster. Stan Wallington was the first Parish Clerk, followed by Jean Burnside, a position she held for ten years until retirement in 1997 when Mrs Pam Tyler undertook the work. The present chairman is Ken Bennison and one of the longest serving councillors is David Tyler having served on the Council since its inception, as well as being a Heath Ward representative on the HBO. Parish Council.Thus it was in 1987 that the Heath's historic ties with Broad Oak, which had existed for many centuries, were finally broken. The population of Hatfield Heath by 1991 had reached 1494 slightly down on that of 1981, which was then 1530. Irene Delderfield had been the village representative on the Uttlesford District Council from 1976 until 1999 when Peter Fuller Lewis was elected to take her place.

In the 1990s the fear of global warming and consequential environmental damage became a national concern resulting in the growth of the conservation movement. However, there were many powerful interests and arguments involved and progress worldwide was slow. As early as January 1950 the Council had nominated certain trees in the Parish for preservation orders and had also proposed a speed limit through the Heath, but in 1988, new steps were taken to protect the countryside. Ditches on the Heath were dug out and wild flowers and shrubs planted. Motor car encroachment had been a problem since the 1930s and the Council, responsible for the management of the Heath, took certain measures, including laying old telegraph poles and digging shallow ditches, with varying degrees of success, to minimise the damage caused. The huge increase in road traffic through the Heath and the expansion of Stansted as part of the overall London Airport system resulted in problems, particularly that of noise. The aircraft noise was eventually monitored through tracking equipment placed throughout the area and all those involved are constantly looking for ways to reduce this nuisance, which since 1995 had been on the increase through the introduction of new airlines operating there.

In 1989 a footpath map was published and in February 1992 the Parish Council appointed Mr F Walsh as village tree warden. By 1998 with the help of Uttlesford District Council he was able to ensure that some 64% of existing trees were protected and that many new trees were planted. In 1995 a Peace Oak was planted near the cricket pavilion to commemorate 50 years since the end of World War ll. Through the kind and generous co-operation of Mr Ian Liddell (Shrubbs) Mr Hugh Scantlebury (Parvilles) Mr Michael Hockley (Friars) and Mr Martin Broad (Benningtons) the Parish Council was able to negotiate new and better access through permissive foot paths on land to the

A History of Hatfield Heath

south around Pincey Brook and to the point where it joins Forest Way, thus creating an enjoyable circular walk of the south-east corner of the Parish. The newly formed Conservation Group formed a working party led by Steve Walsh which undertook clearance work and the erection of gates on the route. They have since been involved in various projects to tidy up the Heath, clear ponds and generally help preserve the environment. The Council was informed by Saffron Walden Museum's natural science department that the Heath to the west of the Church was an area of value and importance in respect of its unimproved grassland site and should be so designated, but at present this has not been ratified.

Since 1970 farming had enjoyed the benefits of the EEC common agricultural policy. However, because of constant modernising of the agricultural industry since the World War II, fewer workers and farm buildings were required. Many farmers converted surplus barns and outhouses for use as industrial units. The high value of the pound in the later part of the 1990s, together with the glut of produce from the Common Agricultural Policy meant once again farmers were experiencing difficult times. They had to reinvest profits and produce the right combination of crops to remain viable, these difficulties being met against a background of public concern over BSE and the use of genetically modified crops. Despite all this modernisation, one old traditional trade remained on the Heath until 1999 where Mr Peter Wilson of Gt. Heath farm operated in the district as a thatcher for over 35 years.

An Uttlesford District Council Village Plan of 1979 had allowed new developments on land at Bentleys and at Tudor Lodge, but no major building work was undertaken between completion of the Lt Heath, Cox Ley and Clipped Hedge in the 1960s and the Close (district council sheltered housing project,) built in 1978 by Tanner & Wickes of Braintree, until the building by Sarbirs of the award winning Beehive Court developement in 1989/91 and the Shaw, West Hayes and Orchard Walk developments of the late 1990s. Messrs Laing, builders of the Shaw estates, also provided the village with the new car park located behind the Countryman restaurant. A project to provide low cost housing was taken up by the District Council in 1992, with two proposed sites listed, this however was later dropped because of cost considerations. The names of the Heath's estates and houses such as the Shaws, Cox Ley and Broomfields came from the lists of fields, woods and houses in the area which were taken from those recorded in the old Tithe maps of 1838. These maps give detailed plans of the village's topography, ownership and its cultivation as it was in the early 19th century and are still a valuable source of historic data even in this age of high powered information technology.

1911 Coronation parade on the Heath.

Edwards' flour mill, soon after conversion from the Brewery.

Harry Gunn at Friars Farm with steam plough.

The Stag decorated to celebrate the Coronation of King George V (1911).

Charlie Halls' garage beside the Stag.

View of Chelmsford Road in the late 1920s, Dunrobin tea rooms on the right.

New houses at Ardley Crescent 1938.

The original Bucks stores before the 1st World War.

View of the Heath from outside Cunningham and Reynolds butchers showing Morley cottages in the background (demolished to make entrance for Broomfields).

Peacock's grocery shop and Post Office.

Cows grazing on the heath showing Churchgate House in the background.

Down Hall as it appeared during Lord Rockwood's time.

Essex Hunt Point-to-Point, first running of Warwick Vase Race in 1937. Valerie Dalton White on Laureate (on left) finished second

Brown Bros. bakers delivery van in the 1930s.

Walter Brown with Friars' dairy milk delivery float.

(V)
Some Buildings of Historic Interest

*"I sing of exploits that have lately been done
By two British heroes called Matthew and John
And how they rode friendly from fine London Town
Fair Essex to see, and a place called Down.
There are gardens so stately and arbours so thick
A portal of stone and a fabric of brick."*

Matthew Prior, famous 18th Century Poet
who spent his last year (1721) at Down Hall under
the patronage of Lord Harley.

DOWN HALL.

The name Down Hall is derived from the Saxon word 'Dun', a hill. In 1540 there was a tudor farmhouse on the site, the messuage (farm) being granted by Henry VIII to William Beuers, Walter Farre and William Glascock, and subsequently purchased by Robert Harley, the Earl of Oxford who in turn gave it for life to Matthew Prior, a noted poet of the day. Prior's first visit to Down Hall was recorded in his poem written in 1715, of which there is an extract shown above. His reference to "A portal of stone and a fabric of brick" was wishful thinking on his part as at that time it was a timber framed tudor farmhouse. He did, however, plan a new house in brick but died in 1721 before it could be built. Down Hall then reverted to the Harleys and was subsequently sold to William Selwin, a merchant who died in 1768, the property then passing to his son Charles who was a banker in Paris.

The original tudor building was demolished in the eighteenth century and rebuilt in plain classical Adam style of brick and stone. In 1870 Sir Henry Selwin Ibbetson (later Lord Rookwood) commissioned the present house. Down Hall house as it exists today, was designed by Frederick Cockerell and built in poured concrete in the Italianate style. It is a very early example of this method of construction.

After Lord Rookwood's death in 1902 Down Hall passed to his nephew Major Horace Calverley who lived there until 1930. During World War I the house was used as a military hospital. From 1932 to 1967 it housed Downhall School for girls. It was then run by Mr G Liddell as a management training centre until 1973 and later St Quen Antiques traded there. Since 1986 it has been owned by Veladail Hotel Group and has become one of the country's leading hotels and conference centres.

LEA HALL.

The Manor of Lea Hall was one of the ten medieval manors of Hatfield Regis and took its name from John de la Lee who in 1306 had acquired estates in White Roding, Hatfield Broad Oak and Matching. In 1473 the lawyer Thomas Unwick acquired it. The house, which is timber framed, dates from the late 16th century and is moated. It has the late medieval form of a central range with cross wings and was originally occupied by the Frank family.

The garden contains, as an ornament, the tracery of a 14th century window originally in a Yorkshire church. At present Lea Hall is the home of Mr & Mrs A Davis.

RYES (or Ryse).

The Manor of Ryes is recorded in the Domesday Book. It is said to be the first possession of Robert de Gernon and was later owned by Ralph de Marcy, Adam de Branktrees and Nicholas Leventhorpe. The earliest Ryes house was on a rectangular moated site and only some brick boundary walls dating from around 1600 still survive. The house was probably rebuilt at this time when held by the Frank family who also owned Lea Hall. In 1638 it was sold to the Stonehouse family and by 1670 it was apparently a substantial building with 20 hearths. In 1677, it was sold to their relative a Dr Woodroff. Later in 1701 the Stanes-Chamberlynes family purchased it. By 1838 it had come into the possession of John Archer Houblon of Hallingbury Place who also owned Lea Hall at the time. He demolished it around 1834 and the present farmhouse dates from that period. During the twentieth century it has been owned and farmed by the Garton family.

CORRINGALES.

The name possibly derives from the holder, Curra the Dane. The original house was called Curra Ings Hall of which there is no remaining trace. A farmhouse was built in the middle of the 16th century on the site. It was converted early this century into three cottages and in 1947 the structure was rebuilt to its present state.

Some Buildings of Historic Interest

GLADWYNS.

The mansion was built in the early 19th century and was first owned by George Lowndes, the High Sheriff of Essex and magistrate, then by the Arkwright family before being acquired, in 1868, by Horace Broke, a barrister and benefactor of Holy Trinity. The Broke family continued the ownership until after World War II when it was purchased by Mr & Mrs Woodhouse. At the present time it is the home of Mr & Mrs D Wilson.

ONGARS.

The present farmhouse was built around 1550 but has been much improved and extended by recent owners. The site and surrounding land dates from a much earlier period and was called Ongar Hundreds. In 1881 the farm of Ongars amounted to only four acres, the tenant being John Pamphilon who was also the tenant of Lea Hall farm. At this time the house was occupied by a farm labourer. During the 1930s it was owned by Mr D K White and Gloria White and is at present the home of Mr & Mrs McKerrell.

THE OLD BARN.

This timber framed building dates from the late 16th century and was originally a barn attached to Ongars Farm. In the 1930's it was owned by Florence Desmond, a famous actress and comedienne of the time. It was reported by the present owner Mrs Enid Kerr that a previous occupant was Lord Rutherford, the Nobel Prize laureate, who first observed atomic transmutation by particle bombardment. Details of previous owners no longer exist as earlier deeds of the property have been lost.

BEEHIVE COTTAGE.

Beehive Cottage was built around 1710 and was one of five thatched cottages built at that time. The only other still in existence is Clipped Hedge Cottage. It was originally part of the Barrington Hall estate and was sold to John Witham in 1827 and descended through two generations of Withams who carried on a business of corn and meal chandlers, as well as running a small grocery shop. It was sold in 1889 to a Mrs Button of Hatfield Broad Oak whose son, John Button, started up a business of harness maker. He married Susan Witham in 1903, who had lived there fourteen years earlier. Their son, also John Button, continued the business and lived at the cottage until 1962.

A History of Hatfield Heath

GIBSONS.

Gibsons, situated at Ardley End, contains parts which date back to the 15th century. It was extensively rebuilt during the tudor period at which time the central chimney was inserted. The first traceable owner was John Dowsett who lived there in the first half of the 16th century, but the Dowsett dynasty had probably lived in Hatfield Heath earlier during the 15th century. Gibsons was a working farm and at its largest was 125 acres as recorded in the 1871 census, owned at the time by Barnard Matthews. Following his death Gibsons became part of the Down Hall Estate and was sold in 1920, to be eventually purchased by a London butcher, George Sweetland, in 1926 and, in 1931 by the Gilbey family. It was sold again in 1956 to the Dalton White family by which time the land had shrunk to 53 acres and was no longer a working farm. Subsequent sales of land to Friars Farm have reduced it to its present 20 acres.

TRADE AND INDUSTRY IN HATFIELD HEATH

Until the twentieth century the main trades and businesses in the village were associated with agriculture and the day to day needs of the inhabitants. According to census returns, in 1861 the population was 622, of which 132 were agricultural labourers, the total number of houses being 124. By 1891 the population had remained relatively stable at 635 but the number of agricultural workers had fallen to 74. This as a clear indication that with increased mechanisation along with the agriculteral depression meant that farming was becoming much less labour intensive in the last decades of the nineteenth century.

According to the Post Office Directory of 1882 there were the following tradesmen on the Heath:-

James Bacon	Baker
Harry Bowyer	Builder
Thomas Cooper	Butcher
George Harris	Baker, Grocer and Post Office
Aaron Hawkins	Coal merchant and Ironmonger
Thomas Mills	Shoemaker
Stephen Nash	Shoemaker
William Perry	Blacksmith
Henry Sullins	Brewer and Maltster
Walter Vale	Agricultural Machinist
Richard Wentworth	Wheelwright

Some Buildings of Historic Interest

John Witham   Shopkeeper
Walter Witham   Cattle Dealer

In the 1892 directory also appeared:

John Button   Harness maker
Edmund Foster   Threshing machine proprietor
Charles Mott   Miller
Charles Perry   Shoeing Smith
Jane Perry   Druggist
John Roberts   Stonemason

In addition to the established tradesmen, there were also a considerable number of journeymen. These were craftsmen who lodged in the village from time to time and included bricklayers, basket makers, thatchers and carpenters.

Brewing came to the Heath in the following way: Peter Sullins, born in 1780, was the innkeeper of the Cock at Hatfield Broad Oak, and in fact lived there for the whole of his 82 years. In the 1861 census he was listed also as a farmer and maltster. His son Henry who also lived at the Cock was managing the whole business, as his father was 81 years old by this time. Peter Sullins had a house built on the Heath, which was completed in 1863 and called Little Brewers. (It is now the 'Hatfield Haven' home for the elderly). There is a tablet built into an end wall bearing the monogram P.S. and dated 1863. However there is some doubt as to whether Peter ever came to live at this house but Henry and his wife left the Cock and moved into the newly built house.

The building opposite in the Stortford Road was already in existence as a maltings when Henry took it over and by 1870 he is listed in the directory as a brewer and maltster. In the 1871 census he is also shown as farming 108 acres. The marriage of Henry and Charlotte proved to be childless and in the 1886 Trade Directory he had handed over the business to his nephew Peter who promptly appointed Henry Mason as brewery manager. Six years later in 1892 the business was sold to Capt. Charles Wardle who was listed in the 1895 directory as a brewer, Peter being listed as a farmer. It changed hands again a few years later and the new brewer was Gerald Bonham-Carter. Brewing ended in this building around 1900 and it thereafter became a steam mill. It is likely that the brewery, which was a comparatively small operation, just supplied local inns and beer houses.

A History of Hatfield Heath

THE WINDMILL.

The date of construction of the Hatfield Heath mill which stood on the left hand side of Mill Cottage, looking south, was about 1841 but on the tithe map of 1838 a circle marks the site. It was built as a brick tower mill with a domed cap, four double shuttered sails and an 8-blade fantail. The mill was originally owned by Ephraim Davy who had also worked the Down Hall mill (destroyed around 1840). Subsequent millers were Simon Mumford, Henry Stokes, Charles Mott, Charles Matthews and Daniel 'Dusty' Day. Charles Mott during his occupancy installed a portable steam engine as an auxiliary power source housed in a small wooden shed adjoining the mill. The main function of the mill was to produce flour for the local bakeries, but the miller also provided a service to local housewives who brought small quantities of corn gleaned from the harvest fields, the flour produced being used for home baking.

The owner of the windmill at the turn of the century was A Oliver & Son, who owned the and operated the steam mill on the Bishop's Stortford Road in the old brewery building. In 1909, although the windmill was in working order, a decision was taken by the owners to demolish it.

THE GLASSWORKS.

During World War II a glassworks was in operation on the site of what is now The Hunters Meet and what was then part of Great Heath farm. Eton Glassworks, whose main factory was at Leyton in East London, was owned by the Childs family who established the works to manufacture medicine bottles and hand blown fire extinguisher phials. The factory employed several local people but in 1951 it moved to Bishop's Stortford before finally closing down in 1958.

SARBIR DEVELOPMENTS

This Company, whose offices are now housed in the old vicarage, started its life as a partnership between Brian Sargeant and Dick Bird (hence Sarbir) in 1961 with a capital of £40, all of which was spent on the purchase of a 1946 Ford van. It became Sarbir Developments in 1962 and in that year received its largest order which was to build a paddling pool for Enfield Council. In 1966 the Company acquired 'Stonedash' near the village hall as a centre of operations, at the same time purchasing the old established Hatfield Heath firm of EH Hockley for the sum of £1. In 1990 the Company moved its offices to the old vicarage and now has plant hire branches in Harlow, Cambridge and Kings Lynn. During the 1990s Sabirs had received both national and local awards for their conversions and residential site developments.

THE PUBS

THE STAG. (Formerly the Bald Stag)

The present building dates from the early nineteenth-century. This inn was for many years a tied house with the Harlow brewers Chaplins and was later owned by Barclay Perkins. From 1862 to 1906 the publican was Aaron Hawkins, who was also a coal merchant and sold agricultural machinery. In the 1861 census he is also listed as a blacksmith. In the 1920s, Mrs Halls looked after the pub whilst Charlie Halls ran a coach and taxi service and also sold petrol and carried out repairs.

THE WHITE HORSE.

The White Horse is an early seventeenth building and has been recorded as an inn since at least 1779. From the 1850s the pub had a succession of long serving landlords including Edward Miller, Israel Mann and Alfred Little. In the 1920s the publican was Thomas Claxton. The current landlords are Tony and Hazel Harriss. The old garage was thatched and was originally a farm building constructed at the same time as Beehive Cottage, but it was burnt down in a severe fire in 1923.

THE THATCHERS. (Formerly the Wagon & Horses)

The building dates from around 1580 and was originally a farm barn later converted into four cottages. In the early years of this century it was altered to become a public house. The present landlord is Nigel Kendall.

THE FOX & HOUNDS.

This establishment was located at the junction of the Chelmsford and Dunmow Roads. It was a purpose built pub and traded from the 1870s. In the census of 1881 the publican was a John Sawyer who was also a general dealer. Like many other pubs in the area it was a tied house owned by the brewers Hawkes & Co of Bishop's Stortford whose business was sold to Benskins of Watford in 1898. The building has been the home of the village magazine printers P.B.M since 1992

this village have passed under her care and as a mark of their affection and respect, parents and children subscribed to present her with a dinner service for which she wishes, through these columns, to return her sincere thanks. She received also from the Managers a peridot and pearl brooch in token of their esteem.

Miss Abbott, too, has left us to take a place in a School near her own home, and her place has been taken by Miss May Coote.

WEDDING.
Oct. 12—James Henry Wilkinson and Sarah Jane Roberts.

BAPTISMS.
Sept. 26—Edith Elizabeth Everald, daughter of Harry and Isabel Lucy Broke.
28—Winfred Annie, daughter of James and Ethel Maud Victoria Francis.

HEATH PUBLIC LIGHTING.
A meeting was held in the Institute on Oct. 2nd, at which Mr. D. Day was re-appointed lamp-lighter for this season. Several of the posts were reported to be insecure and it was decided to put up some new ones. The balance sheet is appended:—

Receipts.	£	s.	d.
Balance from 1911—12	3	8	2
Mrs. Broke	1	0	0
Mrs. Calverley	1	0	0
Mr. W. MacLelland Blair	1	0	0

Per Mr. Rogers:

	£	s.	d.
Mr. A. Hockley	0	2	6
Mr. E. W. Vale	0	1	0
Miss B. Griggs	0	1	0
Mr. W. Vale	0	1	0
Mr. W. N. Rook	0	5	0
Mr. C. Sapsford	0	1	0
Mr. S. Day	0	0	6
Mr. Langstone	0	1	6
Mrs. Blatch	0	0	6
Mrs. Eaton	0	0	6
Mrs. J. Brown	0	0	6
Miss Blatch	0	0	6
Mrs. Hutchins	0	0	6
Mr. W. Matthews	0	0	6
Mr. J. Matthews	0	0	6
Mrs. Jarvis	0	0	2
Mr. Search	0	0	4
Mr. Turner	0	0	6
Mr. C. Mills	0	1	0
Mr. W. Brown	0	0	6
Mr. E. Rogers	0	1	0
Rev. R. C. Jude	0	2	6
	1	3	0

Per Mr. E. H. Hockley:

	£	s.	d.
Mr. M. Stuart	0	1	6
Mr. D. Day	0	0	6
Mr. G. N. Back	0	1	6
Mr. J. Butler	0	2	6
Mr. Mills	0	1	0
Mr. E. Smith	0	1	0
Mr. Perkins	0	0	6
Mr. E. H. Hockley	0	2	6
Mr. J. Button	0	1	0
Miss R. Hutchin	0	1	0
	0	13	0

Per Mr. M. Cunningham:

	£	s.	d.
Mr. G. Trickey	0	2	6
Mr. S. Nugent	0	2	6
Mr. Coleman	0	1	0
Mr. M. Cunningham	0	2	6
Mr. Bowyer	0	2	6
Mrs. Martin	0	2	0
Mr. M. Fisher	0	5	0
Mr. King	0	2	6
Mrs. C. Martin	0	2	0
Mrs. Burbrook	0	2	0
Mr. Robertson	0	5	0
Mr. Harrison	0	2	6
Mr. E. Perry	0	1	0
Mr. C. Perry	0	1	0
Mr. Nash	0	1	0
Mr. Sedgley	0	1	0
Mr. A. Hockley	0	1	0
Miss Bawn	0	2	6
Rev. H. de V. Watson	0	5	0
	2	4	6
	£10	8	8

Expenses.	£	s.	d.	£	s.	d.
Mr. D. Day, lamp-lighting 98 nights at 7d.				2	17	2
Extra lamp, 53 nights at 1d.				0	4	5
				3	1	7

Mr. E. H. Hockley:

	£	s.	d.	£	s.	d.
Five new glasses to lanterns	0	3	3			
New lamp complete	2	10	0			
				2	13	3

Mr. J. Button:

	£	s.	d.	£	s.	d.
61 gal. oil	2	2	8½			
3 yards wick	0	0	9			
17 lamp glasses	0	6	8½			
2 washers	0	0	3			
				2	10	5
Balance in hand				2	3	5
				£10	8	8

H. DE V. WATSON,
Hon. Treasurer.

Parish Magazine report on the Heath public lighting account November 1912.

The Womens Institute prize winning float for 1935 Jubilee celebrations (King George V) outside Hockley cottages.

Parade of children at one of the early Hatfield Heath Festivals

The Stag Darts Team 1950s

Village outing on Mr Halls' Stag bus 1953

Hatfield Heath Football Club 1952-3 in the season in which they won 4 championships.

Hatfield Heath Cricket Team outside the new pavilion 1966.

Hatfield Heath from the Sheering Road, Duplex oil lamp in the foreground with the Trinity Hall annexe on its original site on the Heath.

Ancient Order of Forresters outside Trinity Hall during the 1930s. The old tin annexe can be seen on the right on the picture

(VI)
The Village Organisations

'It was the earnest wish of my wife Lady Eden, and it is mine, that this little effort may be the means of adding to your knowledge and recreation and increasing your happiness. I shall be fully rewarded if you do all in your power to make this Institute successful.'

Lord Rookwood. The opening of the new Library and Institute.
23rd November 1900

THE ROYAL BRITISH LEGION AND THE ROYAL BRITISH LEGION WOMENS' SECTION.

A Hatfield Heath Ex-Service Men Association was formed in November 1926 with Capt. Powell elected Chairman, there being some 69 members initially registered. The first Armistice parade was held that year although, since 1919 services had previously been organised by both churches.

Following a visit by Major Hussey of Ipswich on 12th January 1928, members agreed that the Association should become the local branch of the British Legion with Col Dalton White the first President, Capt. Powell chairman and Col. Stoddart secretary. Capt. EN Griffith was elected vice-president in 1929 and in 1933 became president, a position he held for over 50 years. The branch incorporated the villages of Hatfield Broad Oak, Little and Great Hallingbury, White Roding and Sheering and very soon the social side of the branch was well established. A women's Section was formed in September 1929 with Mrs Dalton White as president and Mrs Griffith chairman. Their standard was dedicated on 20th July 1938.

The branch was active during the Second World War with fund raising, socials, darts and board games, most meetings being held on Sunday afternoons. In 1947 Capt. RE Bloxsome was elected Vice-chairman and played a very active part in local Legion work after the war. Along with Capt. Griffith, Mrs Griffith and Mr and Mrs R Dix he was later awarded the Legion Gold Badge.

After the war Mrs Lillian Burton became Women's Section chairman and Mrs Griffith became president, a position she held until her death in 1970 when her daughter Mrs Madeline Barraclough succeeded her. The present holder of the post is Olive Mays.

A History of Hatfield Heath

Ernie and Eva Dean were both very keen Legion members and left a legacy to the branch, which has considerably assisted their funding over many years. The branch was honoured in 1946 when the newly appointed standard bearer Arthur Wilkinson paraded at the first Royal Albert Hall festival after the war and repeated this again in 1971 before being awarded the Legion Gold Badge in 1977. Since then the current standard bearer, Mick Saban, has also had the honour of carrying the branch standard at the RAH in 1992. Both Mr Saban and his wife Sandra, chairwoman of the Ladies Section, have represented the branch as standard bearers in many Legion events both locally and nationally. The branch, together with the Women's Section, has a joint membership of over 100 and still maintains a very active social side involving an annual dinner, outings, dances, garden parties and shows. Many of these activities were organised by the branch secretary, Ernie Field, and from 1991, by Jim Coe. Currently Peter Waterman carries on this good work along with Sandra Saban. Peter's sister Sylvia Carey is the present secretary of the Women's Section.

Norman Mead of Gt. Hallingbury succeeded Capt. Bloxome as branch chairman in 1985, members acknowledge, however, that Roly Perry is the true 'chairman' for his unfailing assistance with branch logistics. Don Foster has held the important position of service secretary for over 15 years and Ivan Wybrew is both Branch and service treasurer. Frank Delderfield was branch president for many years up to his death in 1999. Florrie Wilkinson, a former standard bearer, was awarded the Ladies Gold Badge in 1998 for her long and devoted service to the Legion cause.

The branch prides itself on its support of the most important activity of the year, namely that of collecting for the national poppy appeal and in this has an excellent and consistent record. Robin and Pauline Woods have for many years been the hard working Poppy Appeal organisers for the branch. Hatfield Heath and District Womens' Section dedicated their new standard at a parade service in 1996 and the new Hatfield Heath & District branch standard was dedicated at a similar service in 1997. In 1998 the men's branch celebrated their 70th year with another impressive parade which was attended by many standards from Essex and from Hertfordshire together with the Deputy Lieutenant of Essex, and Sir Alan Haselhurst MP as well as County Officers and Chelsea Pensioners. The branch also had the honour of receiving, both in 1998 and 1999, the Livermore Trophy given to the most efficient small branch in Essex.

The Village Organisations

THE WELCOME CLUB.

A club for the seniors of the village was formed in 1952. Although there are no records to say why, we know that the club was disbanded the following year. Two years later Ralph Dix was asked to re-form the club and at a successful meeting on April 18th he was elected chairman. With him on the committee were Mrs Dix, Mr Button, Mrs Margaret Hockley, Mr & Mrs P Day, Mrs Sedgley, Mr G Hutchins and the Rev. Milne. It was agreed that the name Hatfield Heath Welcome Club would be adopted and that the club would meet on the third Tuesday each month - as it does today.

The inaugural meeting took place on 21st July in Trinity Hall and took the form of a social evening. About 40 members were present and were entertained by Mrs Want and the WI choir with Mr Patmore singing solos. Mr & Mrs Day together with Mrs Jones provided refreshments. A grant of £10 was given by the Essex Old Peoples Welfare Association to help start the club, later a rummage sale was held which raised £34. At the Christmas party that year Mr Wickenson supplied the presents. The club has always been fortunate in the support it has received from local business and other people and organisations in the village.

There are a number of references on record as to how cold it was in Trinity Hall and in February 1961 the meeting was closed early as the temperature did not rise above $52°F$. In the following year the meetings moved to the school by kind permission of Don Foster the headmaster. However, there was no china available so each member contributed 1/- so that this could be purchased. In April 1963 the members were invited by the Takeley Over 60s Club to watch the Queen and Prince Philip as they drove from Stansted Airport to Chelmsford Cathedral to distribute Maundy Money. At the next meeting Miss Clara Coleman brought in the coins she had received at the ceremony. Eric Halls' coaches with Olive Mays in attendance played a major part in club activities, transporting them to the seaside and various functions. Helen Dix and Lou Hermitage were frequently called upon to provide entertainment. Mr Eardley ran the bingo sessions and Dorothy Search organised the food each year for the Christmas party. Gwen White raised a lot of money for the club through a sewing group held each week in her home.

On the 28th March 1970 the clubs oldest member Mrs B Sapsford cut the tape at the official opening of the new village hall. At that time Mr Dix was voted president and Mrs Hockley became chairman, a position she held for ten years ably assisted by Mrs Letts and Mrs Standring.

The club celebrated its 25th birthday in 1980 when Mr Dix in his 90th year welcomed over 80 members and guests to a party. Mrs Dix cut a beautiful cake. In 1977 Jean Piercy became secretary, a position she still holds and Doris Wright is the long standing treasurer. During that time Mary Halls, Hilda Ely and Robin Parkinson have all had long spells as chairman. Each year the club enjoys a garden party at 'Willoways' the home of the secretary. In 1999 the club was able to welcome Tony Jenkins as its new chairman and is once more ready, at the beginning of the new Millennium, to play an important role in village life with monthly meetings, outings and parties for its members.

THE WOMEN'S INSTITUTE

The Women's Institute was formed in July 1924 after an address by Mrs Cecil Parker of the Essex Federation. Mrs K Carson of Lea Hall was elected president and Mrs Buck, Mrs Du Cane and Mrs Murphy vice -presidents. Mrs Cummins was the secretary and Mrs Dix treasurer. By the autumn membership had reached 103 with meetings held on the 2nd Tuesday in Trinity Hall, the first talk was entitled 'Folklore'.

In the summer of 1926 a successful fete at Gladwyns raised funds for improvements to Trinity Hall. Over the course of the next few years many fund raising events were held which included whist drives and dances and performances by the choir. In 1930s the lectures included 'Essex History' and 'in house' competitions such as 'The best child's lunch for 6d', 'The best present for a lady, costing 1/-', 'Knitting on matches'! and 'The best article made from waste'. At the National Bakers Exhibition in 1931 Mrs Pyle won a prize and locally each year the Institute would enter exhibits in the North Weald Show. The Institute was to organise a successful campaign for the improvement of village sewage disposal in 1935. In May 1937 the group won first prize in the decorated lorry competition at the Coronation celebrations. Later, in 1938 the Heath hosted the Group conference but the September branch meeting that year had to be cancelled owing to severe cases of polio in the district.

At the outbreak of war no September and October meetings were held but the Institute was able to give valuable assistance in these months to the Invasion Committee and help in the operation to evacuate mothers and their children from London. In 1940 a local Womens' Land Corps was formed, run by Mrs Herald, to assist on the local farms. This good work was to continue throughout the war with the formation of a Produce Guild, which included canning and preserving of fruit and vegetables. Mrs Goddard and Mrs Sayer ran this operation and Mrs Kilpatrick was in charge of horticulture and this included the sowing of seeds given by the people of the USA. This work also involved the collection of natural herbs and hips from the hedgerows. These were sent to Messrs Allen & Hanburys for processing.

In 1942 2055lb of jam, 1688 cans of fruit and vegetables, 203 bottles of fruit and 545 jars of pickles were produced by Institute members and a market stall was started in 1943 at Mrs Goddard's home at Clipped Hedge. A great deal of fund raising for many war efforts were also undertaken by members with Mrs Trundle and Mrs Slade appointed as salvage stewards working under instruction from the Dunmow District Council and with the help of the Guides, Cubs and Brownies. By this time too the subject matter of the talks had changed to reflect the war years and titles included: 'Influence of the Press in War', 'Wartime in the Garden', 'Making the most of oneself', 'Vegetable Meals' and 'Music for Blackout Evenings'! During the war period Miss Harris and Mrs Sayer were the presidents Mrs Tribeck and Mrs Dean secretaries and Mrs Buck the treasurer.

The meeting in May 1945 was a very significant one as it was held on VE Day and members listened to Winston Churchill's speech on a portable radio and then attended a thanksgiving service in Holy Trinity at 3.30pm. The salvage operation was later closed down and the remaining income given to the Welcome Home Fund.

Members soon got back into routine after the war with outings and new speakers. Most outstanding of those were given by Richard Bright of the BBC on 'Drama in the Air' and Fred Streeter on Gardening. The winter of 1947, however was the worst on record and greatly added to the difficulties in running the WI Fraulein Bocrawlrawf, a visitor from Germany, attended the March 1948 meeting to see how the Institute ran its affairs so that a similar women's movement might be started there. Miss Landon who accompanied her was a most distinguished visitor having been decorated for her Red Cross work in Germany. Community work in the village was not forgotten either when the branch played host in 1966 to a group of handicapped people from the Newham Borough. The WI raised money needed for a bus shelter erected on the Heath and helped with the fetes run to raise funds for the new village hall and later in 1969 the Hatfield Heath Festival.

The Institute was able to start a drama group in 1956 under the direction of Jean Foster, their first play being 'The Sitter In'. Also in that year a large exhibition of member's work was held filling both sides of Trinity Hall. At this time both the choir, under Joy Faint and Ruby Hole and the drama group were very active attending festivals, services and producing plays. Some interesting visits were organised by the committee to the Cadbury, Frenlite, Lucozade, Key

A History of Hatfield Heath

Glass and other factories. Members also took part in tennis and bowls tournaments and ran a keep fit group. Throughout its existence the Institute has raised considerable amounts of money for various charities and also has been a regular and successful participant in annual area competitions including the Streeter Cup for flower arranging and the Great and Little Hallingbury flower shows (WI Section)

For many years Mrs Guy Wright of Little Hallingbury Hall was an active member and hosted the annual garden meeting. To celebrate the Golden and then the Diamond anniversaries of the local Institute, dinners were arranged which were attended by many guests. In 1990, to commemorate the 75th birthday of the National W I, members designed and produced a tapestry which is now displayed in the village hall.

Over the years since the World War II Mesdames I Liddell, M Selby, M Hockley, C Elliott, R Wright, L Belchamber, J Piercy and D Osbourne have served as presidents. Mesdames Bogie, Greaves, Faint and Ayliffe have been competent treasurers.

It is sad to record that the Hatfield Heath WI closed in 1998 after 75 years. A village group known as the Heath Ladies has now taken its place.

THE PRE-SCHOOL GROUP

Hatfield Heath Pre-school has been in existence for over 35 years. The Playgroup was started in the mid 1960s by Jane Newbold and Barbara Etchells. After an inspection by a rather fierce lady from the District Council the go ahead was given and it was first registered as a playgroup on 3rd February 1964. Hatfield Heath was soon at the forefront of providing playing provisions for 2-5 year olds. Earlier Mrs Delderfield had organised mother and baby afternoons in the village. The Playgroup's meetings were held in Trinity Hall until 1969. This building proved to be inadequate in many ways for the accommodation of very young children. The Group moved temporarily to the Congregational Hall while the new village hall was being built. On completion the Group returned to the village hall which has been its home for the last 30 years.

The Playgroup started life providing play facilities for 12 children initially on Monday mornings and later Thursday mornings with Mrs Cadogan Rawlingson, Mrs Smith the policeman's wife and Mrs Holden joining Jane Newbold and Barbara Etchells. From those early days it has grown to five mornings a week for 30 children at each session and two afternoon sessions for four-year-olds with around 50 children on the register. Margaret Lines, who started as a mother helper in 1970, became leader and manager in 1982 and is still supervisor. Margaret Edwards has also spent many years assisting. Many of the children attending in the past have since married and their own children are now attending the Pre-school Group.

Throughout this time each child has received a free drink of milk at each session financed by the Government. In 1964 milk was 1s-6d (7.5p) but is now 40p per pint. The annual insurance premium in 1964 was £1 now it is £105. Hatfield Broad Oak challenged the Heath Playgroup to a pancake race in 1974. It was such a success that it has become a popular annual event and now includes teams from Little Hallingbury and Sheering playgroups as well. The Group was renamed Hatfield Heath Pre-school Group in 1995 and became a charity in August 1998 at which time the management was transferred to a committee of parents.

The Pre-school now has stringent annual checks by the Social Services Inspection Unit in Chelmsford and regular OFSTED inspections by the Department for Education & Employment, whose reports have been excellent.

THE FOOTBALL CLUB

One of the very first recorded sporting fatalities occurred on 10th March 1567 in a football game at Branton Mead, Hatfield Broad Oak when Henry Ingold of White Roothing collided with Thomas Paviott in a challenge for the ball. Henry did not get up and by midnight he was dead. The Heath Football Club, fortunately have not had that experience but was believed to have played its first game as far back as 1894. Records show that the club made a formal start in competitions just after World War I. One early report from 1920 records a game between the Heath and a team captained by Mr E Bonham Carter. The report continues that a Heath player handled the ball in the penalty area, a penalty was given which then resulted in a 4-3 defeat.

The club has had several grounds, playing first behind the White Horse on land next to a gravel pit. When a right back, after a sliding tackle near the touchline, fell into the water filled gravel pit it was felt to be the time to move on to a safer venue and therefore, in 1923, a field owned by Farmer Millbank near Clipped Hedge was used. Before World War II the ground was resited in a field at Town Grove. In 1939 this field was ploughed up to assist the war effort and it was due to the foresight of Howard Pyle that a piece of ground at

A History of Hatfield Heath

Bentleys Common was purchased from Mr Hart. Howard set about preparing a pitch, which could be used when hostilities ceased. The club used this ground from 1946 to 1986 when a move was made to the present pitch at Calves Meadow.

The Club started again after the war with lots of hard work and fund raising carried out by many village people. In 1948 the AGM. was attended by 48 people. The annual sports fete and flower show contributed much needed finances to the football & cricket clubs and was always enjoyed by all. The ground at Bentleys saw very large attendances for village football sometimes with gates of well over 200 people. One memorable match on Boxing Day 1946 saw the Heath challenge the Prisoners of War Eleven. A huge crowd of villagers and prisoners queuing for entry at one point stretched back from Bentleys to the Post Office! They saw a very strong German team with several internationals in their ranks run out resounding winners 11-0.

The decade of the 1950s was the most successful in the club's history. They were regular finalists at Rhodes Avenue, Bishop's Stortford for league cup finals sometimes playing in front of over 1000 spectators. In 1952 the club won four trophies namely: the Bishop's Stortford & Stansted Premier League and Challenge Cup the West Essex Border Cup and the Bishop's Storford Charity Cup. In 1956 the club repeated the League & Cup double. At Bentleys, about that time, they would attract 200 or more fans and in local derbies against Sheering and Takeley even larger paying gates were known. On away matches the well-known sight of a Hall's coach turning up at the opponents ground would normally mean a hard match for the home team. There were several brothers playing for the Heath about this time including Bob and Roy Nicholls, Bill and Fred Bruty and Bert, Roy and Derek Search. Other stalwarts included Bert Long, John Roberts, Frank Mercer, Ron Dedman, Herbert Maskell, Les Wilkins and Ron Jones. In the 1960s Hatfield Heath also won the league's sportsman's trophy and was invited to play inside Chelmsford prison. Over 500 inmates watched the game and this time the club got its revenge on internees winning 5-1. Hatfield Heath can claim to be one of the most successful junior teams clubs in Essex, winning trophies in each of the decades from the 1920s. These achievements were coupled with an excellent reputation for sportsmanship and hospitality. In May 1996 the Club's ground was featured in the national press when the famous 1966 World Cup goal in which Geoff Hurst's shot hit the bar and dropped over the goal line was re-staged there with the German goalkeeper of the final, Hans Tilkowski, and the original orange ball. Both former players signed autographs there and had time to praise the condition of the Heath ground. Many excellent players and officials have served the Club over the years. Bill Bruty, Howard Pyle, 'Sugar' Perry,

The Village Organisations

George Brown, Wally Day, Ian Kettridge and Bob Jerrard all helped to shape its success over many years, whilst most of these also served on League and County committees. Mr Bruty was a very much respected member of the Essex F.A. and 'Sugar' served the Club in various capacities for more than 40 years. Norman Cunningham, Alf Patmore and Eric Halls before the war and Howard Gunn, Les Trott, Bert Search, Roy Howard, Stan Barker, Alan Wilkinson and Cliff Moore all played senior football for Bishop's Stortford, Sawbridgeworth or Harlow. Howard Pyle (The Peter Pan of Heath football) was a prolific goalscorer and was still playing in his 50s for the Club. Reg Howard played for the Heath for many years and was also a well-known long distance athlete. In more recent times Bill Gleed has been a stoic defender as were the Lines brothers Ian and Andy. John Deamer, Stewart Perry, Ian Bennett, Andy Claydon and Michael Bamber all have long service as Heath players. The present chairman is John Deamer snr who has held this position for many years, and the team has been managed by Mike Briscoe since 1991.

The Club's most recent success came in 1994 when they won the Bill Bruty Cup. (The Premier Division Trophy). They knocked out Alemite Athletic (Essex Junior Cup Winners), North Weald (Essex Junior Trophy Winners) before beating Anmol 6 -1 in the Final with Neil Jones, great nephew of Bill scoring the last goal. David Pyle, grandson of Howard, maintains the family tradition as a regular team player.

For years the committee banned Sunday football, however two sides from the village, Pegasus in the 1960s and Heath Hall Park in the 1980s started playing on Sundays with some success and eventually all players were allowed to play on that day.

Hopefully, the Club is in a position in which it can look forward too more success at football on the Heath and with it lots of fun.

THE CRICKET CLUB

The founding of the club is not accurately known. The first known recording of cricket being played was a match between the Marrieds (Benedicts) and Singles (Bachelors) played in the village on Monday 26th June 1865, resulting in a win for the Singles by 3 wickets. A match played on Tuesday 22nd September 1868 between Hatfield Heath and Hallingbury at Hallingbury is the first known game against a local village. Hatfield Heath scored 78 and 127 and Hallingbury 40 and 44. This may have been a club side or just a team of villagers. Information is very sporadic but other local villages were playing

A History of Hatfield Heath

earlier, so there is a strong possibility that Hatfield Heath was as well. It is certain that cricket was being played by a village side in the following years from match reports in local newspapers.

The village team in those early years went under a variety of names, HH Juniors, HH Coffee Tavern and HH National School Cricket Club. It was not until 1884 that a reference is found calling the team, Hatfield Heath Cricket Club. On the departure of the vicar, Rev. AE Beavan, a well-known local cricketer, in 1885, it was reported 'The establishment of cricket clubs in the village was due to Mr Beavan, who has taken a personal interest in the game'. Though cricket had been played before the Rev. Beavan's time, perhaps he established it on a firm footing as a club.

In September 1920, the Cricket and Football Clubs combined to form the Hatfield Heath Athletic Club under the presidency of the Rev. EA Du Cane.

There was no cricket played on the Heath itself in those early days. In 1880, 1881 and 1885 matches were played on the 'Back Fields' in Hatfield Heath by kind permission of Stephen A Pamphilon, whose family lived at the time at Lea Hall. In 1882 a match was played in a meadow lent by Noah Griggs, who lived at Little Heath farm and in 1892 a hearty vote of thanks was given to Mr Cooper, who owned the butcher's shop (next to The Countryman) for the use of the ground for so many years. The 'Back Fields' were behind The Stag and The White Horse, even in 1946 the Broomfields area was still known as the 'Back Fields'. On January 27th 1894 the following announcement appeared in the Herts & Essex Observer - 'Lady Rookwood has kindly started a subscription with ten guineas for the draining and levelling of the Heath, 'that the lads may have somewhere to play cricket, etc.' Mr H Broke has also given five guineas and the work in now in progress'. Work may not have been in progress at that time for on November 3rd 1894, the following announcement was made, 'The Cricket Club have decided to level part of the Heath so as to make the ground available for next summer's cricket'. The earliest reference to cricket actually being played on the Heath was in June 1897.

The number of matches played in a season in the 19th century was low, though a result was normally obtained. Both teams usually batted twice and if the second innings was not finished then the result were decided on the first innings total. In 1892 the club played 5 matches, winning 3 and losing 2. By the 1950s they were playing 30 or more matches in a season with varying degrees of success.

The Village Organisations

There was no cricket played during World War I, but 1914 saw a full season's games, however it was not until 1919 that matches were resumed. In the 1920s though there would have been little traffic using the Matching Road, there was the hazard of telegraph poles alongside the road, almost onto the cricket square, which must have caused one or two problems. They were not removed until the 1950s.

In early 1944 a bomb dropped onto the cricket square, completely devastating it. The square was reinstated after the war but matches were not played on the ground until 1949.

Matches had been played until 31st August 1940 with only occasional games being played during the war against local teams of servicemen. Competitive cricket was not resumed until 10th May 1947 with an away match against White Roding, still the opposition on the first or second game of the season.

Cattle and sheep grazed the outfield with the grass being occasionally cut by local farmers. A scythe was used to cut the playing area and the immediate surround. There were times though when the grass in the outfield was tall enough to hide a person lying down and runs had to be restricted to six when a ball was lost in it. In the mid 1930s land drains were laid across the ground by Mr Henry Newman and water was laid to the square in 1954.

Mr B Pyle donated money for the club to purchase their first mower, an Atco. In about 1936 a second mower was purchased second hand from Bishop's Stortford Golf Club, a horse drawn one that the Club converted to be pulled by a modified Chevrolet car. It was kept in a field owned by Mr Bowyer of 'The Laurels'. Gangmowers, for cutting the outfield, were not purchased until after the war, along with the first tractor. For many years right up to the 1970s the wicket was rolled with a granite roller that had been shipped from Cornwall by train and needed six people to pull it. In current times Richard Barnett, John Gunn and Peter Graves have the use of more modern equipment for ground maintenance.

The start of the season in the 19th century was not until about mid to late May and matches were often played during the week, though Saturday was the most popular day. No trace has been found of Hatfield Heath playing games in the village on a Sunday in those early days. It was not until 1949 that the Club requested permission from the Parish Council to play on a Sunday. This was granted so long as matches ended before evening service, when the church bells rang.

A History of Hatfield Heath

Before the age of the internal combustion engine, opponents were local village or town teams, though in 1893 the Club played Fyfield, no doubt travelling by horse and trap, or perhaps bicycle. From the 1930s until 1973 Halls' coaches took players to away games.

Matches between Marrieds and Singles seemed to be a popular fixture for clubs. In 1870 such a match in the village attracted 17 players in each side, so there was no shortage of potential players. In later years this fixture has turned into the under and over 35's.

The 1950s and 60s saw the Heath returning some notable achievements, most seasons winning more games than they lost. The 1970s and 80s saw very mixed results with the club usually losing more games that they won.

The earliest known officers of the Club were in 1890 when Edwin A Cates, a master at the National School, was the secretary, the vicar, Rev. JL Green being the treasurer. In 1892 Cornelius Nash was captain and J. Button the secretary. Mr Nash played cricket for many years, as did Edward Harris who followed as captain in 1896 and 1897. The vicars all seem to have been prominent in village cricket since at least 1871, they all played for the club. The Rev. TW Reynolds was Chairman in 1897.The longest serving officer has been Mr Howard Pyle who has been associated with the Club for most of his life. He was President from 1953 until 1999 and has been associated with the Club for 73 years, both as a player and an officer.

Until modern machinery could maintain a close-cropped outfield and wicket, the scores were invariably low, rarely exceeding 50. It was possibly in the game played against Hallingbury in 1868 that Hatfield Heath scored more than 100 for the first time, though in 1887 a team from Gladwyns scored 229 against a Heath team. Possibly the first century scored against the Heath was made by a C Skeet who made 122 playing for Great Hallingbury in a match on June 30th 1900. The lowest recorded score was made by Matching Green on 7th August 1871 when they only scored 6 runs, nine of the players getting 'ducks'. The Heath has had their own low scores, on 14th June 1924 they only scored 7 runs against Takely with seven players getting 'ducks'.

In 1953, Bert Search scored 106, which may have been the first century scored by a Heath player. In the previous week he had taken 9 wickets for 7 runs, still a club bowling record. In 1961 his brother Derek Search scored 136 runs against Hockerill. This remained the highest individual score until Ian Perry scored 140 not out against Little Hadham in June 1996. The best recent bowling

The Village Organisations

performance was in 1993 by Jason Cowley who, against the Eastons, took 9 wickets for 27 runs. The best all round performance was that of Graham Chapman who in 1980 scored 737 runs and took 79 wickets in that season.

The changing facilities were rather primitive, a tree adjacent to Mill House had nails in it for hanging coats there being no hut or pavilion for changing. A garage at the front of Mill Cottage owned by Mr Ted Hockley was eventually used until a hut was erected on his land.

The Institute had acted as the headquarters of the Club, meetings being held there until in the early 1960's the club decided that a proper pavilion was needed. Regular whist drives held in the Institute, organised by Herbert Maskell and Stan Turner, helped to raise £800/900. With this amount to hand, the decision was made to start the process of obtaining permission for a building. Howard Pyle with the assistance of Ted Hockley, Norman Cunningham (Chartered Architect) and members who were professional in their trade including Bob Nicholls, Derek Search, Cliff Moore, Fred Luckey and Stan Barker set about building the new pavilion. The final cost was met by the Club with a core of members erecting it and even making many of the internal fittings. CH Gosling granted the Club the use of 1.33 acres of the Heath at a peppercorn rent of 15/- per year for a period of 47 years. The pavilion was officially opened on Sunday, 1st May 1966 by the Club President, Howard Pyle, with over 100 people attending. Mr Pyle was presented with a commemoration plaque for his work on the project. The toilet facilities were added in 1968. Herbert and Stan still continued to raise money by running bingo sessions every Saturday evening in the new pavilion.

How fundraising was done in the very early days is almost unknown, though in January 1895 the 'Hatfield Broad Oak Blackamoors' gave an entertainment in Trinity Hall from which £3 was made available to the Cricket Club. From 1950 to 1970 the Football and Cricket Clubs organised a summer fete in the field at the rear of Bentleys, raising money together and using common ground equipment. In the 1990s an annual quiz evening has been the main fundraising activity.

Refreshments were taken in a number of locations in the village. On July 5th 1880, teas were taken in a booth provided by Henry Sullins, a local brewer and farmer. On July 18th 1881 tea was taken after the game under an oak near the vicarage and in 1882 refreshments after some games were taken in the vicarage. In 1886 lunch was taken at The White Horse. Following an afternoon match on Wednesday, 28th August supper was taken in The Stag. Again in 1897 the season was brought to a close with tea in Trinity Hall.

Teas were later taken in The Fox, then run by Mr and Mrs Bonsey, before transferring to the Institute and provided there for many years by Dorothy Search and a team of lady helpers.

THE GARDENING CLUB

In September 1882 an inaugurating meeting of an annual show of vegetables fruit and flowers open to cottagers in Hatfield Heath, Matching and Sheering was held at Down Hall. It is known that at least three shows were held, alternating between at Down Hall and Gladwyns. It has not been established as to whether this Society was the original Gardening Club or just the beginnings of the annual produce show now held in September.

The present Club began in October 1973 when Mr Frank Walsh called a meeting in the Village Hall to explore the possibility of starting a Gardening Club. Thirteen people attended that meeting and decided to set up a committee. Mr Walsh was elected chairman, Mrs Doris Mead the secretary and Mr Richard Barnett the treasurer and membership secretary. Monthly meetings were arranged from January 1974.

The first meeting was held on Wednesday, 23rd January 1974 in the then Congregational Church Hall when 54 members joined. By the end of the year the membership had increased to 80, with annual fees being 50p for a single and 75p for a double membership. By 1978 the membership had increased significantly and a move had to be made into the Village Hall to accommodate the increased numbers.

The Club had originally only considered holding monthly meetings with a speaker but even before the end of 1974 there was demand for horticultural goods and the club therefore branched out into selling seeds, composts, fertilisers, etc. This obviously needed capital and it was decided to raise £250 by asking members if they were prepared to lend the club £10 per member as an interest free loan. These loans were eventually paid back from profits made from commercial sales and increased membership subscriptions. In 1978, the Coronation Jubilee year, Irene Delderfield promoted a competition for the best front garden in the village and asked the Gardening Club to provide the judges. This idea was taken up by the club holding an annual garden competition of members' gardens, both front, back and vegetable. Enid Kerr presented a trophy for the best flower garden. Later, in memory of our second chairman, George Brown, his family presented a trophy for the best vegetable garden.

The membership of the club fluctuated over the years with more members coming from surrounding villages and towns but always remained healthy. In the 1990s with the advent of gardening centres the interest in 'do-it-yourself' gardening declined and, although the club has remained viable, the practical side has diminished with fewer members growing their own plants from seed.

HEATH PLAYERS

For at least a hundred years the Heath has entertained itself with concerts and dramatic productions, in the early years usually under the auspices of the churches and schools. The earliest recorded dramatic activity is found in the Herts & Essex Observer of 1922 which were dramatic renditions and songs in a style popular at that time. In September 1925 a pageant written by local headmaster Ralph Dix and entitled "Women through the Ages" was performed at Gladwyns by members of the Hatfield Heath Women's Institute supported by some male members of the community and local brownies and guides who represented the future. Among those portraying famous women of history were Mesdames Butler, Buck, Button, Barker, Claydon, Dix, Davies, Gunn, Hockley, Harris, McLeod, Nairne, Rogers, Roberts and Trundle.

During the 1939/45 war a group called The Hatfield Heath Players "did their bit" entertaining the village and at the same time raising money for wartime causes. A concert during "Warship week" raised £15-14-6 and the newspaper recorded that "many were turned away from the doors because the hall was full to overflowing." In November 1941 the Players performed a triple bill of "The Bride," "A Day's Good Cause" and "Mystery Cottage." 1942 saw the Players raising money for Alan Gardiner's Fund (Vicar of Holy Trinity) which was for Christmas boxes for soldiers. After a gap of five years the Players appear again giving two performances of three one-act plays. Members of the Hatfield Heath Players included R Dix, M Hood, O Jackson, M Llewellyn, I Jones, W Monck, J Horsey, D Fitch, R Savan, Miss Ward and Mesdames Muddit, Searle and Buck,

The Heath Players of today grew, or were born, out of the WI Drama Group, a thriving female group started in the late fifties. In 1967 Charlotte Schroeder, a skilled linguist, invited a young National Theatre actor whom she had been coaching for a part, to speak at the annual WI members meeting. The actor, Christopher Timothy, readily accepted the invitation to be the surprise speaker and gave the meeting a lively and amusing glimpse of his experiences in front of and behind the scenes of a prestigious theatre company. Following his talk he was introduced to Jean Foster, the driving force behind the WI

Drama Group and in conversation expressed his enthusiasm for starting a "mixed sex" amateur dramatic society. From this conversation grew the Heath Players. The first production was advertised for May 16th, 17th and 18th 1968 to be held in Trinity Hall, but the three nights became two as the Friday night performance had to give way to a prior booking - a dog show!

Chris Timothy at that time lived near Matching and several founder members were from Matching Green, notably the secretary and treasurer, Barbara and John Williams. Later their daughter Vicky, was a member of the Youth Group. Early rehearsals of the production "Night Must Fall" were held in the Marriage Feast Room at Matching and at the first read through the Players needed one actor to complete the cast. The headmaster, Don Foster, pinned a notice on a tree in the school playground; "Actor required to play Inspector Belsize in Night Must Fall". A newcomer to the village, John Taylor, presented himself thus completing the full compliment of actors for the inaugural production. The play was staged in the old Trinity Hall familiarly known as "The Tin Tabernacle" The drama critic of the Herts and Essex Observer wrote of the first performance "Both the group and the venue were new to me and I must confess my heart sank when I entered what must surely be, from the outside, one of the dingiest looking tin sheds in the broad acres of Essex. Slatted wood seats of incredible hardness did not do much for drooping spirits, but when the curtains parted there was that surprise - a beautifully detailed bungalow interior solidly constructed and expertly lit, peopled by actors who both knew their lines and could deliver them with conviction." The next full-length play "Doctor in the House" was performed in 1970 in the splendid newly built Village Hall. This was followed by a revue "Ha! He! Sh!" (Hatfield Heath Show) designed and produced by Chris Timothy and Peter Lines.

During their early years the Players were fortunate to acquire a wonderful wardrobe mistress, Gladys Melville, who had worked in a West End theatre costuming famous actors, a lighting expert, Peter Lines, who combined a wide knowledge and enthusiastic interest in every aspect of theatre work and assistance from a variety of professional technicians with whom Chris Timothy had worked in television.

January 1972 saw the advent of what was to become an annual pantomime, Aladdin, written by John Crocker. Most of the subsequent pantomimes were written and directed by Chris. From this time support for the Players increased, with standards backstage, on-stage and front of house improving and audiences enjoying purpose-built tiered seating, a luxury unknown to most amateur companies. A vibrant Youth Group was now re-established, a reincarnation of a group that had faded in '68, meeting weekly in the Institute. In 1972 the group's entry in the Drama Festival "Ritual for Dolls" directed by Peter Lines achieved its best ever result of 95 marks only two marks behind the overall winner for that year. From this time the company became more adventurous in its choice of plays reflecting a growing confidence, notably "Billy Liar" directed by Chris Timothy and "A Day in the Life of Joe Egg" in 1974 directed by Rona Savident. These plays provoked much comment from audiences both favourable and condemnatory with letters to the Players and the Village Magazine.

A Music Hall Troupe was formed in late 1974 adding to the Players varied repertoire. By 1975 the Music Hall was in full swing, ranging far and wide and raising money for many local charities with its performances to audiences attired in any Victorian apparel they could lay their hands on. When performing in the Village Hall a Bangers and Mash Supper with "Cyril's Secret Sauce" was served, Cyril Hackett being the chef on these occasions.

By 1975 growing membership and support accounted for an income of £1157-95, a considerable amount at the time. 220 Costumes valued at £600 were stored at Gowrie house while storage and workshop facilities were made available to the group at Corringales thanks to the generosity and support of Commander Reay and Mrs Robin Parkinson. The Heath Players has always had the support of families in the village amongst which were the Buckle family, Stella and Graham Smith and family, the Parishes, the Collins, the Lines, the Taylors and the Penkeths. Other longstanding supporters from the early years were Grace Clark and Spencer Robey.

The growing membership of the Junior Heath Players brought greater participation from their parents and whole families were active both in front and backstage in productions, especially in pantomimes. The Players staged a spectacular Cinderella in 1976 with "the most beautiful coach seen in an amateur production." Designed by Barry Walsh it appeared on stage as if by magic, the stage floor sinking for it to roll smoothly through the open doors carrying a radiant Cinders off to the ball. The script was written by Chris Timothy while Peter Lines and Wendy Bundy directed and produced. Peter Lines also wrote the music which was performed by resident pianist Sheila Collins with Peter Baker, bass, and Keith Clark, drums. The Report in the paper remarked on the "sumptuous costumes" by Gladys Melville.

The departure of the Timothys in 1976 left the Players slightly shocked but strong and healthy. Chris's letter to the group on leaving said: "I try to avoid making distinctions between pro. and amateur drama, but make no mistake it is a little more than being paid and not being paid. Of course you are doing it for fun, but never forget the audience who has paid to watch you. The prime consideration is attitude, and surely it is more satisfying and thus more fun to do this the best way you know no matter how much hard work, so that finally, the audience do get their moneys' worth and you do have fun!" During the next year the programme of plays, pantomime and Music Hall continued with enthusiastic energy. There were also several entries to Festivals and the introduction of Studio productions of one-act plays over one or two evenings.

The Heath Players celebrated their tenth anniversary in 1978 with a brilliant production of "Oh What a Lovely War" directed by Rona Savident. This was well received by audiences and critics who reported on "a successful presentation of an aptly chosen piece of theatre." The run was followed on the last night by a grand buffet with a beautiful celebratory cake. Highlights of this year included an exhibition of stage props and costumes, mounted for the Village Festival by Gladys Melville and other members displaying the glory and glamour of Panto and Music Hall; a presentation of "Lord Arthur Saville's Crime" directed by Brenda Jones and with a stunningly elegant set designed by Barry Walsh and a tenth anniversary repeat of Aladdin. Janet Tomblin of the Herts & Essex Observer wrote "Remembering the previous Aladdin it is amazing to note how this group has progressed in eight years. The polish, the precision and, above all, the spectacle could never have been forecast in 1971." a suitable finale for the Heath Players tenth year.

The following years were a time of expansion in many aspects of the theatre. The group adopted a written constitution, mainly the work of Peter Lines. Panto and Music Hall took to the road which involved an incredible amount of effort by many volunteers in transporting scenery, costumes, lighting and the attendant paraphernalia involved in such ventures.

At this time the Players had a membership of around 80. New directors were taking over and amongst the vital backstage crew were very competent "props" people, "sound" men, and an absolute army of "set" movers during pantomimes. In 1979 the name of Mark Ratcliff appeared in the list of set construction and stage staff. Twenty years later he is still to be found working backstage and in 1990 was even seduced into appearing "on stage" in the production "Bedroom Farce." The group continued to benefit from the splendid sets designed and painted by Barry Walsh while the thriving costume hire business run by Gladys Melville from Gowrie House played an important part in keeping the Heath Players solvent.

The Village Organisations

In 1982 the Players performed "She Stoops to Conquer" and as a good contrast "I am a Camera" directed by Brenda and Allan Jones. The latter was also performed in the Studio Theatre in Harlow, the only time the Heath Players had performed there apart from one-act play festivals. In the same year the Junior Heath Players displayed their considerable talents in "The Amazing Eiffel Tower on Wheels Show" written and directed by Janet Lees, one of the senior Players. It was much enjoyed by players and audience and was described in the local press as "a vibrant original production." The following year saw another first for the juniors, a successful production of "Noah" directed by Stella Smith. The Youth group were also greatly involved in the Musical "Smiling Through" directed by Allan Jones when the Players combined with the Roydon Players for the performance in what proved to be an enjoyable and lasting collaboration. The Musical director for this show was Sheila Collins. Sheila was again musical Director for the highlight of 1984, a splendid presentation of "The Wizard of Oz" directed by Stella Smith and Steve Foster. The play involved no less than forty characters including The Munchkins and as many people backstage. Ian Collins, keyboards, and Pip Pyle, drums, joined Sheila to provide the band for another "wonderful spectacular show." (Herts & Essex Observer).

In 1986 the Players revived "Robinson Crusoe: and welcomed Chris Timothy back to a performance of the show that he had written and directed ten years earlier. The following year the Players joined with Roydon again to present a musical "All for your Delight" directed by Allan Jones. This satisfying worthwhile venture had a cast of twenty-three combining talents from the Heath Players, Harlow Theatre Company and the Roydon Players. Four set constructors and a vast amount of backstage help was mobilised for this brilliant show which had six performances spread over two weeks in the two villages. Meanwhile members of the Youth group joined with other young people in a production by Carol Jepps of "Joseph and His Amazing Technicoloured Dream Coat" performed in the church. Nigel Owen, the organist trained the young singers in this delightful one-off event.

Although the Heath Players put in much hard work the 1988 Pantomime "Puss in Boots" seemed not to have as much verve and vitality as usual. During the following years there seems to have been a lull in the Heath Players activities. Longstanding, stalwart members Douglas and Gladys Melville moved to Edinburgh while Barry Walsh married and moved away and Brian Edmondson retired to Devon. Much front and backstage help was no longer available, a sad reflection possibly of the increasing pressure of work leaving less time for other activities. All this led to the need for simpler sets and

A History of Hatfield Heath

presentation, with actors having to work with more imagination and improved technique. This was greatly helped by skilful lighting and sound technicians who can create miraculous effects assisting actors in whatever representation is required.

After quite a long break the Players made welcome return in February 1990 with the comedy thriller "Bone Chiller" directed by Renee Joyce using both junior and senior members of the group. The following autumn saw "Bedroom Farce" directed by Jean Foster with three double bedrooms and beds invitingly made up in front of the audience. This brought forth gasps of surprise and comments such as: "Oh well, if its boring we can have a nice lie down" and "If you drop off tonight you can snore in comfort!" The lighting men didn't miss a cue, so important in this play.

In 1993 the Village Hall was decked out with railway memorabilia for a production of "Off the Rails." directed by Jean Foster. This was hailed as a "hilarious comedy for all ages with excellent performances from the actors, notable ones from Steve Foster as the stationmaster and Mark Ratcliffe playing a tipsy Scotsman." Tickets were clipped by an uniformed official and snacks were available from the Station Buffet (run by Margaret Lines) during the interval. The programmes were adapted from railway timetables.

Christmas came early in 1994 in November with a performance of "Season's Greetings" by Alan Ayckbourn with its mixture of comedy and thought-provoking undertones. A lovely Christmas tree decked the set and entertainment was provided by Uncle Bernard's Puppets. The Group, by now proficient Ayckbourn players acted the play well. The Players became more adventurous in 1995 in its choice of play "The Lion, the Witch and the Wardrobe." directed by Jean Foster. It was simply presented yet quite magical, with wonderful lighting effects by Peter Lines, evocative sound and music by John French and excellent performances from the whole cast and backstage performers. The Herts & Essex Observer reported "An Evening of magic and a lesson for any amateur group on how to stage a wonderful production, all you need is imagination." Another play for children, Alan Ayckbourn's "This is where we came in" in 1996 proved challenging and exhausting for the actors who were never off the acting area, becoming different characters at the whim of the malicious Great Aunt and Uncles. (the story tellers) Goodness finally triumphed with the banishment of the "Greats" by the hero Fred. Again excellent performances from the cast were admirably supported backstage.

In a departure from the normal winter production in February 1998 was the presentation of two one-act plays performed in the Institute. "The Laboratory" directed by Mark Ratcliffe and "Lunch Hour" directed by Dave Perry were much enjoyed by audiences. This was followed in the autumn by the classic play by Moliere, "The Miser" directed by Jean Foster. This received a glowing report in the local paper; "A super cast with not one weak character...... a splendid performance from Steve Foster as The Miser."

In their 31st year the Heath Players are still a "force to be reckoned with" on the Amateur Drama scene. Founder members Jean and Steve Foster are still vigorously involved with the company. Long-standing members Simone and Dave Perry are still acting and supporting in divers ways while Peter Lines still "lights the way." One time Juniors Ian Ketteridge (now father of three) and Adam Thompson still make appearances as seniors. Other members including Carol Morse, (Clarke) Patrick Roberts, Jane Jackson (Hackett) and Barry Walsh still practice and promote their enthusiastic interest in their present homes.

THE BRIDGE CLUB

The Bridge Club originated in Little Hallingbury in 1971 when Tony Henderson and Bob Parker founded a club at the Village Hall, some members joining from Alick Gibson's bridge tuition classes. Soon membership increased so that a permanent venue became necessary and the club established itself at Hatfield Heath, first in the small committee room, then the Institute for many years and finally in the main Village Hall.

The club has currently about 70 members and meets every Wednesday. It is affiliated to the English Bridge Union and to Hertfordshire as its home county. The club offers a varied programme for the more serious Bridge player but in a most friendly atmosphere and players come from Hertford, Hoddesdon and Harlow as well as the outlying villages around Bishop's Stortford. Club players have represented the county and play in Essex, Herts and Harlow Bridge leagues. Some members have also been successful in national competitions. The club runs an event every year as part of the Festival week and also runs a charity event in January in support of the Welcome Club. An annual match against Bishop's Stortford BC is held in December involving 16 players from each club, with Hatfield Heath winning the first match in 1975 and also winning the last 3 contests.

The highlight of the year is the Heath Cup, an invitational teams event held on the 3rd Sunday in October. Teams come from a radius of 40 miles around Hatfield Heath to play in the event that is nowadays fully subscribed early in September. 128 players provide testimony to a well organised, but highly enjoyable event on the calendar.

A History of Hatfield Heath

THE BOWLS CLUB

At the beginning of the 1990s an indoor bowls club was formed, meeting at the Village Hall. This was largely due to the efforts of Dave Jordan (the first Chairman), Brian Evans, Tony Gibbar, Norman Woodford, John Smith, Ken Butcher and Brian Bland. The success of the afternoon sessions was due almost entirely to the enthusiasm and drive of the late Hodge Goodwin.

Since the beginning, the Bowls Club has contributed around £3000 per year to the Village Hall Trust, through subscriptions and match fees and has done much to foster a greater community spirit within the village.

THE WEA

The Hatfield Heath Branch of the Worker's Educational Association was started in the early 1960s with Don Foster as chairman and John Payne as secretary. At the present time, the secretary is Cliff Burnside but Don Foster has remained chairman throughout. Pauline Kemp, as treasurer, is another long serving officer of the Branch. Hatfield Heath is only one of many branches in the surrounding towns and villages and these operate under the general administration of the Essex Federation of the WEA. In 1998, Hatfield Heath had the honour of hosting the County AGM in the United Reform Church hall.

The Branch normally organises two sets of lectures each year: one in the Autumn and one in the Spring. Lecture courses usually take the form of one evening lecture per week spread over a period of ten weeks and have covered a wide variety of subjects, these are selected by members and have included such topics as: archaeology, family history, local history, natural history, music and philosophy. For many years lectures took place in the village school but in more recent times the branch has met in the URC's well appointed hall.

AND IN CONCLUSION:-

This little book has now reached the end of its journey. Our recorded inheritance began with the like of the Celtic Cunobelin, through the Saxons, Sigeberht and Edward the Confessor, Normans, William the Conqueror, Alberc de Vere and Robert de Gernon, the great families of Barrington and Bruce, Morley, Rich and Selwin. Some of the people living here today are able to trace their ancestry back through the centuries, where many of those have contributed to this rich story, which is the history of Hatfield Heath.